# THE WIDE ROAD

ISBN: 978-0-9823387-4-2

Original cover art © Nancy Blum
Cover & interior design by HR Hegnauer

Belladonna<sup>*</sup> is a reading and publication series that promotes the work of women writers who are adventurous, experimental, politically involved, multiform, multi-cultural, multi-gendered, impossible to define, delicious to talk about, unpredictable, & dangerous with language. Belladonna<sup>*</sup> is supported with funds granted by the New York State Council on the Arts, the O Books Fund, donations, and by the generous hosting of Dixon Place.

State of the Arts

NYSCA

Versions of some sections of *The Wide Road* first appeared in *Aerial* (edited by Rod Smith), *In Camera* (edited by Chris and George Tysh), and *Tessera* (edited by Lianne Moyes). The authors thank the editors of these journals for their early support of the project.

Distributed to the trade by
Small Press Distribution
1341 Seventh Street
Berkeley, CA 94710
www.SPDBooks.org

Also available directly through
Belladonna Books
925 Bergen Street, Suite 405
Brooklyn, NY 11238
www.BelladonnaSeries.org

<sup>*</sup> deadly nightshade, a cardiac and respiratory stimulant, having purplish-red flowers and black berries.

# THE WIDE ROAD

## CARLA HARRYMAN

## LYN HEJINIAN

BELLADONNA* 2010

Late one afternoon, we find ourself wandering in our city, the site from which we have long regarded the distant horizon. It is always changing. We notice that we have been distracted by many days and minutes, many trees and malls and continents, many radiants and radicals, many names and figures of many men, children, women, goats——and that we have been walking in silence for such a long time that we have reached the ocean, where we encounter a little drama, a rescue in which someone is saved from drowning. A plain day has turned into a sad and hopeful one, filled with story and passing time. There is nothing left for us to do now but to return home.

Each morning we swept the threshold at our door until we'd worn it down to almost nothing, a mere undulation, a slight wave. Then the wind swept into the house from under the door. With the wind our story moved forward to a future on dry land, then shifted to another, intimate, sweaty scene. It stroked our legs and our dress trembled on its hook. The scene came to an end and began again. We enter it here, leaving our broken house in a state of ecstasy.

We have left our broken house in ecstasy, traveling out of the city. We walk in a vaporous valley with our bovine heads bent toward the plain where it is said it is possible to measure desire. We can't wait to see the grass that grows there. Our wish makes us thirsty.

       spilled from an empty pan
       the patch of rice
       left behind

       —running to risk
       the rain

Time and again the curly yellow weeds were clawed with clicks by bicyclists who dodged us where we walked, thriving with modesty. Tree and grass seeds scattered in the increasingly firm air. There is no analogous flattened happiness to that of curious and receptive travelers. Indeed, the morning bowed informally to us from the wide road which was filled with things to be coupled and compared.

many thoughts remain
in a soft head

How was it that we could still hear the slurping of deep kisses as clearly as when they first occurred and were recognized as the structure for much that was to come? We remembered our thrill upon discovering, for example, that two halves could be reversed.

we find it delightful
to go to another place
while we still sleep
in this one

one this
in sleep
is still

where will
we fit nips

We wrote these lines with inconsolable dispatch, after leaving the apartment in which we had spent our first night. WELCOME was the official instruction hanging from its door. A stranger had knocked with a deep and sylvan racket just above the peephole at its center, and we, sleepy from our exertions but hospitable in the hope that hospitality would be offered in return, had taken the shiny knob in our fingers and had opened the door.

We could say no more than this:

> in a perfect circle
> rises the warm spring night
> but it gains an enormous length
> before it sinks

Spreading our legs we invited the stranger to enter and make himself comfortable.

> only my shadow
> will come to you
> tonight to beg
> for a little flesh

Shadows harbor the opportunity not missed, and the chance not found, and the change not altered, but they cannot quiet the chains rattling in the deep trough of our drunken hugeness. The trough reflected a sliver moon and horses stood against it with their lips parted. Slowly we said goodbye to the stranger whose shadow came to call in the soft damp ground behind the house and:

> the pine trees somber with Latinity
> against a horizon
> charred by the moon

issued from his Pasoliniesque lips like dawn tumbling on a thoroughbred's flanks.

We wrote: Dear friends, we love you. We are traveling away from you and toward you. We love our pleasure too, and it makes you shy even to think about us speaking. But we hunger for knowledge, that giant mind inside our heated wombs, so we follow the osculant terrain. When tired, we cross our legs and laugh lustily. But sometimes

> we say love
> without you

there is no aim

but our own

swarming voice


which is the widened seam of wandering.


We don't need to assert our autonomy. The flowers tickling our breasts as we lie in a sunny meadow fuse us to the awakening consciousness of more-to-come.


tossed butter

is hard to eat

even so


Today it's sexy for you to never know who we think we are.


Our mortal bones are made up of a hundred minds and a multitude of orifices. These we now apply to our adventures. Every pock in the ground, every blade erected in it, every soft coursing of an animal, every shadow affixed to the daylight, the color of the grit between shoe and foot, the slips of tongue as we prematurely mumble the elements that stimulate future conversations, a shift of balance from left shoulder to right, and the wide but bounded stretch of our audible route fill our senses, so that we were compelled to write:

the sun presses against the ground
look! at our tongues
like separate birds they fly
into a shifting shadow

Though the mind darts from thought to thought without continuity, our postures flow through unnamed but endless positions as we proceed. It was enough to say right foot. Then a whole succession of sensations, from toe to sole to ankle to calf and knee, thigh, and so on, follow, swinging us toward our goal. As for the left foot—it is not a mirror of the right. We are no more symmetrical than a brimming tide or the sky which is scattered over the terrain, and as a result we enjoyed several unexpected experiences.

along the swaying road
we help the sore wind
and point ahead to it
deeply buried in the sun

We travel toward the ocean with empty spider webs wrapped around our face. Morning, afternoon, and night each has its own story.

the preservation of tunes within
the voluptuously emptily
lit room

Every poem is a posture we have tried:

leafy froth of toe
we bite in circles
topples time our flick
we wrestle wrists

legs fly
with other
wave over
screen

our navel light flies
low as search

death slipping finger
up thong
of one

craft over a stormy sea

reach under the breath

sun

salutation

                    curving

         spines


         middling on a stalky ridge
         we butt heads with yarrow blooms


         testicles knot between
         hairs breath and loose
         clothes


One morning Scheherazade's whisper reached our ears on the
wind cautiously charming our necks as we climbed an exposed and
rutted hill. "Even the chill prickling your thighs through coarse
pants is an inducement to continue."


         shaman
         on the floor
         the new moon


"We are watching the plants growing, but we aren't making them
grow," we said as we topped the ridge. Our guest, her ghost,
pointed to the reclining sun. There is the ubiquitous grove. We
settle ourself on a slab of shale. Back home, we might be hurling
cherry blossoms down a chimney to avoid the wrong male.

> even our toes curl
> with discarded shame

In our dream, an ambivalent Dracula licked our arms.

Are we vain to think that such wasted gestures have been pushed aside? In the afternoon, having paid no attention to direction, we get to Rome, still miles away from the yearned for ocean cliffs. "We are an archeologist who speaks too much." But even so the boys on a busy corner don't hear us and grab at us instead. We find ourself sunning, with one boy at each breast, next to the statue of a bombastic lawyer. Halfway on the sidewalk and halfway in the garden, the boys have spread us out so that our head nearly bobs over the gutter and our feet are buried in flowers. The boys have removed our coarse pants and are idly, almost lazily, rubbing us with jasmine vine while they also hold their still-dressed crotches.

> sometimes
> helter-skelter
> but becalmed, deeply
> we are turned from our guest

Below the garden there is a sheltered slope hiding a gentle cavity to which we soon persuade the boys to digress, being in that mortal frame of mind against which time presses through a thin drapery that barely conceals its preciousness and enormous size. "Fuck time," we said, batting at the budding flowers in which we lay. When one hits something, the perfume rises in an instant, and this induces dreams.

> we cannot be interrupted
> crossing the swollen river

This was our dream: We are standing, we see ourself do this, ankle-deep on a vast beach of iridescent pearl sand over which a sheet of shining water lies motionless, like a vast and penetrable mirror tilted very slightly toward the sea. We look down into the water and see reflected there what's between our legs. Reluctant to distort the perfect view of what is otherwise so difficult to see, we lean forward. Slowly we sink closer, down into the cold water and the warm sand below, to suck up the pink and dark object of our study, until the water hangs around our thighs. People on the beach can see us from what would be distance except for a quiver in the air that has flattened and immobilized both near and far in a single plane of diffuse light. A scent before our eyes. We inhale as a large wave washes the rosy shell away.

walking half asleep

a blossom between our feet

unable to be indifferent

we wonder what became of the tree

After lingering a little longer in the shadow of the slope, we return
to the statue of a lawyer and there encounter a tourist who is
hiding his guidebook. We ply him with questions about the statue,
and pretend to yearn for a guidebook, until he is forced to pull it
reluctantly from under his shirt. Its pages are dappled with stains
laid there on purpose as mementos by his inquisitive sisters who
wanted him to remember them and the fact that they had learned
ahead of him everything that he would learn on his trip. Thus we
discover that the lawyer in real life had had an enormous body and
only four toes on his right foot but six on his left. In the statue he is
wearing socks but no shoes, as we learn when we part the branches
of the twin topiary bushes growing at its base.

even the invisible is aromatic

tiny eddies of sound an inch or two long

a huge statue cannot see all of its loneliness

in a garden puddle after rain

It was late on Wednesday morning when we left Rome. We had
intended to get an early start, but we spent several hours in a

market weighing our wet shoes, soap bar, tweezers, extra sweater, travelers checks, notebook, and anthologies, and wondering what could be discarded to lighten our shoulder bag. An old woman with chill white hair came into the market and happily agreed to take our wet shoes to wear after her bath.

> frost upon a city stream
> weeping of a speckled fish
> old hands in the market
> lifting onions

Not wanting to effect the outcome of a labor dispute at the railroad yard, we decided to travel a short way by air, and so we left Rome by the Appian Way in the direction of the airport. It is no fault in travelers to be led astray, and so when we came to an ocher archway dripping with wisteria, we turned aside and curled our fingers over its supple branches. A dusty road led toward some buildings, the buzzing chords of bees resonated in the air, and a tall young man appeared in the distance to beckon to us formally. Then he entered one of the buildings. It resembled a guard house, and as we entered from the sunlight we felt the humid draft and floral odor that hung within. The young man was holding a plastic cross in one hand. With the other, palm up and fingers spread, he motioned toward a stairway going down into the ground. His smile was very beautiful, tentative but not candid. On the wall

above the stairs were traces of words, now illegible. A placard
dangled from a nail on which was spray-painted an arrow pointing
down between two rows of giant feathers and beside it the word
CATACOMBS.

> a touch of sympathy
> is all that remains

At the bottom of the stairs, the man took us by the hand,
intertwining our fingers with his. He directed the top of his plastic
cross ahead of us and turned it on. The beam of the flashlight was
wide, and we could see stretching out on all sides a network
or web of passages, and along them rows of dusty beds scooped
into the underground walls. We drenched our senses in this holy
scene, pressing the dark fabric of our guide's coat for consolation.
He turned in response, kissing our throat, then touching the tip
of his tongue to each eyelid. "We mortals are born to be afraid,"
he said, "but not pathetic," and he directed our attention toward
a particularly deep dirt bed at the end of a corridor to the right.
Eternally expectant skulls looked up at it from the ground, and,
shuddering slightly under his protection, we went toward it.

> love is only semi-blind
> it cannot number the thickening of shadows
> but it sees the pockets that they cast

Every day is not met with pure excitement, robust health, and an approach to travel through virility. It is not always with clarity that we experience our sexuality, clarity being a preference of anticipation's net, a net which catches us askew and sweeps us into a ball before the foot of a giant walking twig with spurs. We call him the underworld Bob. But that was some other time. We anticipate the following days as the sun drifts down below the dry mounded hills. Yet, we are not in that story either (to which we will return when our appetite is great). It is now a morning when we are not woken by water gushing through the irrigation canals on which we sleep. We echo what this day is not, as our more domestic sunshine beams in through the window of our house onto our partly uncovered torso, as if it were a target for the figures of speech floating rudely on the ceiling and finicking with each other's half undress.

> "to move"
> a mental effort
>
> cannibalizes the light

And even the fans of our bath are washed with trembling indecision. Rouging droplets shimmy on our skin in mimicry. We know that we are not always well-loved, but hiding is no remedy.

flocking

with bandits


A very good song is on the radio and heralds our departure.


the signature

of a favorite artist

is the prick

of the gathering flood


"Good-bye rouge-plants and shudders." We walk toward the bend in the road carrying but half of what we need.


driven

sense in sense

relentlessly

close hereabouts

and bestowed


On our body, desire has formed a wordless groove. Thus the body partakes of purposive existence. Life itself is productive, and its elements, which are both the seedbeds and the seed, are nourished and maintained by special essences in the atmosphere. But we could not take seriously the supposed likeness of grass upon the earth with the hairs on a man's head.

> along the road
> stalks, grass
> no braiding
> of their steel

Love opens life's warm seams. Do you realize that we're clothed in skin inadequate to any other destiny? No one was there to hear this question. The mother's breast is still unveiled but no one watches the scene with fatherly interest.

The morning light, forming pearly drops of mist, sprayed against our mouth. We inhaled the heady emanations of the eucalyptus trees whose ragged bark and pungent buttons were drawn into the breeze. A young unhaltered mare approached the trough under the trees nervously, shying with contradictory impulses, prancing backward and tossing her head. Then she thrust her head forward and curled her lips around a column of water deep in the trough beside the fence.

We opened our shoulder bag and wrote in our book:

hidden under our open eyes

the cleft

is coterminous with our destination


We set aside our rifted introspections in order to get to the motel
by nightfall. The shoulder of the interstate is not safe after dark. So
without pausing for thought we found ourself by 8 p.m. facing a
salad bar under an enormous antlered clock at Al's Lockhorn Cafe.
Across the street the reflection of the word EAT from Al's neon
sign was flashing on the windows of the Recluse Motel.


ah! night lights

pushing through to the bed

—almost at that height already


We know that sex is sometimes an escape from other more
indigestible knowledge. The lights flash again and we have no ap-
petite but one. Again, like anyone, we're miserable from the news
of the day.


flapping around the air-conditioned room

newspaper brushes our skin


We kick the sheets off.

legs open

the street


The curtains are drawn a little, and as long as we can see the source
of the rumblings, we can remain relaxed.


herds of jellyfish

surround a waterfall


We succeed within our skin where cars have failed with their
tires. When we awake the air-conditioner is off, the curtains and
windows open. Light. No traffic. Early morning footsteps. We
wrap ourself in a green sheet and brush our yellow black hair until
it beams around our head like a moon. Children's voices draw us to
the window. The children are holding hands in the street between
the diner and the motel swimming pool. "Children, get out of the
street," we cry from the window. "Stay street!" yells a militant two
year old. Panicked for their safety and applauding their audacity,
we rush to the street and scoop them up squirming and twisting
and deposit them on the sidewalk where they run every which way
like crazed lizards until we tackle them again. They delight in this
game but finally relent, allowing us to sit quietly with them on the
ground. Our pale green sheet covers the sidewalk. The children
cling to our necks. They tell the story of Sally who loved them

and made them happy every day but had to close her door to them forever because officials said she didn't have and could never get the right license. "But where are your mothers?" "Cutting down trees." "And where are your fathers?" One little one, pulling on a curl above his ear, says, "My green blocks live in the forest." We find the ground quivering beneath us. Soon we are moving forward, then flying. The children hold onto us as if we are a mast. There is nothing but our little ship and rushing white and gray. Industrial steam or clouds, we can't say. While we are flying thus, the children make up fortunes:

> Blisters, bounties, brothers, walls will not be the same as a boiled egg; welcome the wall

> A cold heart belongs in a refrigerator

> Bed and sleep seem to be necessary but sometimes it is wise to do without; you will play in piney forests, then climb beds and sleep

> Refrigerators offer the best storage for golf balls

> Beware of cartoons in which skunks ignite bombs: ahh mm bomb

Be careful about where you show off what you
know and go to the movies often: a show shows

We exit the show, watching ourself, surrounded by children. We
walk down a pebbly path to a house where we deposit them into
the arms of magical relatives for safekeeping. As we make our
departure, without really marking where we are going so engrossed
are we in discussion, we wonder how Basho could abandon a child
in the woods or Rousseau give his away.

Yet, like them, we cannot but proceed. We project a future we will
wander into, not knowing if the pebbles will be as pleasant to the
touch over time as they are at this present location.

as if dough

covers

the smallest

universe

Man & body. We love one, and *for that reason* we address these
questions to him. Yes, there has been a preface before we ask
our questions, and not a short one, or if not exactly a preface,
then a build-up, because intimacy isn't a received tradition. It's
our invention.

In our preface, delivered on the edge of his chair, we had reached way back. The children we rescued today are not survivors, in fact the babies they were are dead. The repetitious mortality of beloved children is recurrent, so that inevitably someone has to notice it. We are, and will be, inconsolable, we say, intellectually. But you, the lover, do not die so regularly, and that's the reason we come to you for reassurance. We say all this before asking, "Will the land be cold or flat?" and so forth.

He seemed not to be listening, or not to consider the questions interesting. Must we insult ourself with explanatory chaos, a disclosure of desire?

Standing now, withdrawing, we write in our notebook:

> an amateur of natural science
> a body possessed of information

> —around the temple of certainty
> nothing but cloud

Our breasts are unhanded clock faces.

We guard our time carefully and cover them. We are wearing ice-blue lingerie. Also several warm sweaters. Hefting the strap of our shoulder bag, heavy with notebook, checkbook, ID, felt-tip pens, raisin boxes, handkerchief, flashlight, penknife, maps, phrasebook, extra socks, chapstick, binoculars, library card, and a packet of photographs, we turn our right cheek to a dry breeze from the east and head north, in the general direction of Milwaukee.

> midday meadows, ears buzzing with corn
> our outer nature is lazy
>
> our inner nature is active
> the book's best setting

In the middle of the afternoon, we come upon a small shingle cart beside the road parked under a red and yellow beach umbrella at the edge of a cornfield surrounded by a cyclone fence. There is no one around, but the sign over the cart says HONOR SYSTEM and we select one cucumber (at 3 for $1), domestic Swiss cheese ($2.89), string beans (98¢ a pound), and a box of mock-imported unsalted crackers ($1.49), and deposit $5.69 in the small paper bag nailed to the post that supports the sign and the umbrella. Then, munching on the beans (first biting off the tiny stems, peeling off the "string," and sucking out the green for a moment before biting into the bean), we walk a little ways until we find a shady spot in which to rest and look at the photographs.

Our favorite was taken by one of the children. We are sitting on the pale green sheet before it had turned fluid under our tears surrounded by the other children. We have nuzzled the ear of the child sitting in our lap—his ears were like scented magnolia blossoms. He had squirmed, holding a piece of bread in one hand and a small book in the other; butting his head hard against our breast, and biting the bread, he had thrust the book toward our eyes. This was clear enough indication that he wanted to hear a poem:

A little horse
had a big belly
into which he swallowed the sky.

Where is my sky?
cried the rain and the clouds.

Inside the horse,
said a pigeon and a cow.

Little horse, little horse,
said the clouds and the rain,

We think you have
more belly than brain.

The little horse
tossed his pale green mane.

Open your lips,
said the clouds and the rain,
We will kiss you
where you swallowed the sky.

The little horse spread his lips in a smile.
Wider, said the clouds.
Say "please," said the rain.
Wider and louder, they said again
and again.

The little horse pranced
and did as they said.
Ah-ah-ah, said the horse, eye-eye-eye
and out came the beautiful sky.

We adore you, said the clouds
and the rain.

A trap. Trains under horses' feet. Dust slides to front. The sky
palpitates to our projections. "I will react," we say and make

a man spinning around an eye. The eye is the only feature of our "landscape preserved from autobiographical writings"—a terrain that miraculously came (Kathy Acker would say "orgasmed") from the pen of Journoud sometime prior to our trip to Milwaukee. A flat building drops to the ground. We find Journoud preparing the road. An eclectic gunrunner is trying to obfuscate our invention: Journoud? Acker? "Orgasmed"? The road? The gunrunner will fail to discern the invention, to weed it out from borrowed drek. Because

we are Cassandra Persephone Pandora A. Prop

We slide the rifleman's coarse and superficial immorality under our gown. I bet you would like to know about this gown. It is terraced and rumpled on one side, in blues grouping backward into darker hues as it drags. In an ecstasy torment of passivity, we refuse to open our arms. The hand thrashes within the bucket.

dryness and passion
don't mix

said the professor. It is best to take her out of the desert, put on a few pounds, and give out bullets of lust. We raised our hand, since we'd realized we'd been captured and put behind bars. "Will these words suit, professor?"

peach juice

slut

triple


"I can only tell you that dryness is not sexy and I've never heard of
Eric Satie, though a man."

"This can't be the University of Milwaukee!" we exclaimed.

The Professor admitted that it could not.

It was an Institute of Inquiry, though not of Measure. We lay about
with some of the students who were discussing brute force. "This
topic always makes people obvious," said the woman who was
supporting herself with her right arm on our lap in order to lean
more emphatically toward the splendid but rigid man. "We need
immediate substitution," she added.

"You can't improve the world with dictionaries," he said.

"You're right—but you can with airplane tickets," said the one who
had been talking about fishing and was now stirring chowder. "My
own recipe," he said; "a secret broth."

The sea-scented steam condensed on the walls of the room and even the sheets and pillowcover felt slightly damp, as if we had been sweating.

"If no one yields to brute force, it can be very exciting," we pointed out. The interlocking we imagined increased our appetite. There were spoons to go around but not enough bowls, so we shared ours with the man who had caught the fish, sniffing the odor of his brow as he guzzled the soup from the bowl on our lap.

"It only results in stagnation, if no one yields," said the other man.

"Who? We?" Cupping our breasts with our hands we made the familiar jest.

> we desire only you and you and you
> for verification

Later, kneeling in the moonlight on the grass above the brick embankment that held the bend in the river, pouting and spitting we said to ourself the word "cupping." He was delighted, and shouted "Xho!" Then we directed him to say something fundamental and provoking, using the letter L.

Lavinia, Lavinia, Lavinia

Paranoia results from that old religious preoccupation with the smallest detail and with similarities. And traveling as we are, we can't always indulge in self-portraiture, even when we are stark naked and whopping. In fact, much of the time we exceed the pronounced differences between you and us, since they demarcate the biological depths and social heights, reproducing history and producing isolation. Meanwhile, we incite ourself to introspect and expect—is this love? is this theory?—we are not experts of postponement.

> our head is round
>
> such is life
>
> have we not hatched it?

"We can't get that poem out of our head," we said. We are slaves of environment.

Our fisherman is standing just behind and above us on the slope. He embraces us from behind, passing his fingers over our breasts; then he reaches between our legs: he has us in the palm of his hand.

From this elevation, or apparent elevation, we have a remarkable look over a nine-foot high fence into the yard where outdated statuary is stored at the face of an eroded cosmonaut and at 17 arms and forefingers of Lenin.

oh rousing weight
still more tremendous
oh wondrous love!
oh loud applause!


This is true: we are writing on a cloudless sheet of blue paper.


we come closer to facing
the frightening malleability
of gender


Oh. Oh, so. Oh oh. Oh, no. No. This is also true: as we write three shirtless men carry enormous tree parts along the side of the house. One of them is dark and wears a pale blue hat. Another is light with long straw-colored hair and an earring hanging lightly from a delicate ear. The third is responsible, pale, and hulking. We are certain of our third man's role because he stays in the backyard with a saw.

But this window scene of men is only pure distraction from the work at hand: the manufacture of serenity amidst uselessness, noise, chaos, and demoralization. And now, awesome reader, listen to what is not true—a dream—and then we will tell you how we got down from the mountain.

We were sitting in folding chairs, in about the center of a small-sized unembellished public space, possibly half-full of people, watching a movie. The movie had a familiar plot, and we were remarking on the disquieting yet soothing boredom experienced in being able to anticipate the future so readily, when L, C, P, and K entered noisily. The room leaked light through the large moth-eaten curtains covering the floor-to-ceiling windows, so we could see the newcomers quite well: they appeared to be slightly larger than life, as if in a pale fog just before sundown, when the blending of object and shadow and the simultaneous contrast of illuminations and darkness yield a somber massiveness within the landscape. Now, the movie served as a distant overexposed backdrop to the presences of L, C, P, and K. As the red-haired C crossed from the back of the room to the curtained windows, L followed. It seemed that C was looking for an exit. But, upon sensing L, she turned and kissed him passionately. The passionate kisses were repeated as they stood next to the audience like drunken guests at a wedding party. We felt, also, a tinge of desire for the booted L and his remarkable nonchalant poses which we attributed to his many years of theater experience. When C released herself from the embrace, we rose, feeling an almost familial obligation to speak to her. We said, "C, we didn't know that you could attract like that." C looked at us severely, and we knew that we were very small, almost insect-like, as she floated through the curtains to the patio.

The film came to an end. The curtains were drawn, the shabby bare room exposed. We felt that we must rectify ourself, so when C floated back into the room as if it were L'Opéra, we said, "C, we are very sorry that we spoke insultingly, but we did so admire you for being an Artemis." None of this seemed to mean anything to her, and we left the theater with remorse.

Now, the reason we have postponed telling you how we got down from the mountain is that we had to work our way down, and this was very difficult. Anything we could put our mind to we would try, but few people will pay for the work of a mind such as ours, one that does not fear the incongruity of yielding statuary. So we offered ourself up as a gardener. Yet, few on the mountain could afford the luxury. We sometimes went hungry for want of a proper fit. Still,

> it is in the places where things
> don't fit
> together neatly
>
> that we can best insert
> our political will

This political will belongs to the slapstick side of our nature which is so often embodied in the form of a man who himself embodies both wisdom and gluttony in balanced proportions. And it is of him, Candy & Eggs is his name, that we eat when we get too hungry to continue down the steep, sparsely populated, and heavily forested slopes. We lick and suck his sugary fat and sip from his eggy eyes, while he sleeps the sleep of a spellbound material witness. At last we are sick of him and return him to a sitting position, proper to the religious, by repeating our recently acquired Lavinian Chant....

Everybody, meaning the few people of the valley, was there to greet us when we completed the descent. And yet

>we starve
>as we work unnoticed
>through the one
>endless
>source of work

We write, Dear Men, our messiness broadcasts our tendencies, our capacities, but it can't conceal our tendernesses. Go ahead and call us filthy if you will. We have eyes and a tongue, lips and a navel—we are a triangle in perpetual motion. We didn't wriggle down the cliff clutching at pungent warm shrubs, ride exciting slabs of hot slate down the slope of the high meadow, arrest our careening in the glossy mud of the cool creek (we lay for a spell in the stream of water, head on green moss, one leg on the right bank and the other on the left—what enigmas await us in the zone between vegetable and mineral!), climb the trellis at the back of the villa where we were gripped by the thorns of the bougainvillea whose blossoms stuck in our hair, sneak over the roof and around the chimney, and swing down past the windows clinging to the wrought-iron floral grillwork and the edges of the tile cartouche in order to get to this place without getting dirty. But here we are! Be artful, if you will—please clean us.

> almost carnal clods for scrutiny
> almond science sinking
> pillars, pillars, pillars and minerals

The magnificence of many generations goes to sleep. As always Time and Habit and Zeitgeist survive. Much too tired to proceed, we remove our pale pink sandals and fold our legs and sit in a window seat. Gauzy speculations filter through the curtains, until we part them slightly. Live motes swarm in the light. A figure, no larger than a finger on the street, enters the scene. The scene is theatrical but inverted, languid, temporarily unbounded, but local. The sky above the buildings is flowing out—this is simply a characteristic of the color blue—and yet expanding. The words— we hold a book and it is open to page 213—waver ("No wounds their bodies suffer; 'tis their minds that feel the deadly stroke"). All the things in the story are rushing from the street toward their words—because things love their words: "juice," "maddening," "brew," and "not content with this."

> we're made mindful
> by flea bites
> of you

"The plain on which Measured Desire dwells is…," said the old person in the doorway as we departed on the morning of the 23rd, presenting us with a package of sandwiches (sardine, if odors speak) and a jar of artichoke hearts ("the aftertaste of artichoke is the same as the aftertaste of weeping," explained the sentimental but observant old person). There was nothing religious here, and we were pleased to accept the gift.

Just as the road on which one expects to go east branches, one arm to the northeast and the other to the southeast, so a traveler's appetite and the means of satisfying it frequently fail to coincide. "Our parents had the annoying habit of driving past the perfect picnic places convinced that a slightly better one would come up further down the road," we said to the old person, suddenly reminded of our childhood by the smell of the vacant lot on whose foxtails, popsicle papers, yellowing shreds of newspaper, and dogshit the sun was beginning to shine.

"It's going to be a hot one," said the son of the old person. "Want a lift?"

We thanked the old person one last time with shoulder, hands, and tongue and then, refreshed and restless, we followed Glo to his pickup truck.

It was difficult to write legibly while sprawled on the warm torn vinyl in the bucking truck, but we managed to scribble the following lines:

> we indeed seem to deserve our punishment
> we leave each sacrifice unfinished

Surely we are happy.

We deny it. Our very abundance has made us unsafe.

> Finding metaphysics on our folding
> promiscuity is topnotch. Yet
> millions dine tonight atop
> crasser breakthroughs. Some
> people mean what they say
> to each other, folding their cards

to display themselves. Imagine!—
those who buy ornaments handling
money everyday: the historian
will not touch our clothes. Our clothes
that feel matter of fact
only to machines. Their sheen
shrinks within our massively
feminine hands. Diminution cries out—
"Oh, monstrous time, elapse!"
We crave one-twenty-one, you—
salt. And sits on the lily. Back
to back, we the bumpy animal test
our misshapen invention. Eat out
the envelope. Neanderthal clutch.

One theory is that women barely tolerate men. We meditate on
this notion while we pull off the anchorman's socks and shoes and
suck his toes. In this crease of the world we write poems on our
brothers' beautiful asses and give Diana naked lily. But Dick yells,
"You can't love everybody." "When we agree," we say, "you die."

      1) our sex is speech minus sound
      2) we must get to know our resources

Sex is an incitement, urging us to elapse. Or wrap. Or glare. Uninspected, undressed, and unreconciled as we are, we continue to watch for the flickering which had been an anchorman. It is the passage of time that allows us to become moral, and as we wait we watch the wriggling of the sunlight across the floor and onto the futon where we are resting as it expands until we succumb to its elusive but warm pressure on our naked breasts which we call Me and Not-Me.

Just as the tips of bare magnolia twigs make little ovals in the wind, just as the eyes of a frog can see in every direction, just as common gossip wavers this way or that, just as mothers in their sleep hear their babies' crying from all sides and come awake in an instant, just as a horse may be taken to represent certain forms of meditation, and just as desire provides its own genesis and sex its own explication, just so we sprawl in the flickering sunlight.

The sunlight is applicable to our situation, or, shall we say, we make it so.

>           all labor is respectable
>           in the saving

Masturbation is equivalent to a pamphlet.

militants, flirts

in their fortress,

the author

with foamy criteria


Forever!

We thought this when the music ended and the news came on. We saw an island and rioters. Back on the mainland, the President was sitting in a wicker chair, drinking anti-toxins.

We unfolded our map, the one that indicates both depth and elevation, and dumped our money onto it. There was enough for at least one more day, which meant we could leave before the bank opened.

The news was in its final stage as we settled into the rented car, the jock and the meteorologist were interviewing a mercenary, the meanings of the words "climate," "climax," and "calamity" had merged, and we departed.

The noise of a car and the sense of motion are always conducive to introspection.

We knew we were angry about something; many things point to it. As for the anger itself, it is located sometimes in the torso, resembling a dahlia rooted in the stomach but blooming against the ribs where they form a cage behind the breasts, and sometimes it's in the skull, like a copious sweat worked up by an idea. Or so it seems upon introspection.

One has to introspect *something*.

> assuming abrupt control, assuming
> magnification, the authentic Aphrodite
> is relatively large
> and ambiguous

You titles of men, do not touch us! Not the samurai but the scowl produces our choice vocation, our literate licks. However, we confess for the sake of our love of the camel and its open sway that sometimes, while havoc has hold of our priceless repose, we call upon Joyce's multiple styles for proof that we can say modestly, "once sprawled in the flickering sunlight." We do. For the love of *Arachnida* and sticky lines. Or is it that we had just written "within the grip of" amidst the clamoring semi-tropical shrubs, clasping ourself to ourself in the dampness?

            obscure Macoute

            participation in

            Haitian election


Dampness, thicker than rain, fades within our pungent, dilettantish
mouth tasting of affinity and finality. The end and the beginning of
money meet. Obscure Haitian—


            not fitting

            or water

            funny bursting

            under earth


            earth fitting

            water

            not under or

            funny

            bursting


            or under earth

            fitting bursting

            not funny water

earth

water

under

funny

or

not

fitting

bursting

not water

earth


or bursting

under fitting

funny


Surfaces get us out of the car. The bribe is paid to Legba in satin.
Mysteries are negotiated. Earth water under funny. That ocean may
be only an engine turning over the wet skin of air:


fixed election

silences

Port-au-Prince

An envelope is sent to the field where an original goddess pees on an ear of corn. Our radio softens the air with its distant voice of public acts. In the street a man, tool belt slung around his hips, approaches. A little farther on, a more domestic fog organized by fences, house, and shrubs embellishes a quince the mechanic's mate prunes.

> whether *durant*
> or *pendant*
> Duvalier's zeal

We have to admit that we are inextricably cut off from and connected to landmarks. Self-consciousness stalks our every sensation with the sound of *stop*—minus sound. Falls and mixes with the penetrating rain.

> a jagged adrenaline
> regulates
> the breath

In another order or arrangement, which is outside, a low military plane breaks the sound barrier. Pliers clank against the face of the car as the mechanic rests his head against the engine pillow.

the goddess
averts her eyes


The next day, among all the excited managerial effects of a prolonged return, we find a man


who's glum
in light
of our self
portrayal


Our temperature has such authority we never feel it. Nonetheless, when we have occasion to think of it, as now, feeling the man's warm right hand as we shake it, we are reminded that we live within its effects. The rich get richer. Our mother sent us to the university to learn this, although possibly she didn't realize it at the time. This is what is known as nature, according to this gloomy man. He refuses to take off his yellow shirt, although the light is strong and we are getting warmer and warmer.


We are feeling more and more complete. You are an unfinished person, we say to the man. We can say this smugly; it leaves us naked.

Naked, our breasts are eyes.

"This is what is known as direct seeing," we say to the man as we back away from him.

"Okay, okay," he says, and for a terrible moment we think he is going to hit us.

> apples, apples,
> policy, policy,
> autonomy matters
> most

When we were five or six, sitting on our knees in the back seat of the car, riding at night in a rainstorm through Alviso, gazing backward at the road behind us, we saw less than we see now. The rain on the side windows described remarkably slow but persistent narratives suspended in drops making paths that intersected or effaced faces drawn with mouths opening and eyes that never closed. They put us to sleep. We didn't see Alviso because we were asleep.

The whole body is built of heads, and every head has its face.

"The drawing of the Cyclops in the book is wrong," we said to the incomplete man, who had finally taken off his yellow shirt.

> scope and drone
> people need good jobs
> our babies laughing
> incompatibly

In the sensuous world of politics, while thousands of people wriggle in anticipation of a debacle or a sudden change, thrilling to the announcements of policies which guarantee the prolongation of the sexy human disasters about which they always need information, partial knowledge is very stimulating. We constantly think of that horny foreign doctor Faustus, lamenting that he'll never know enough.

But he vows to "conjure in some bushy grove, And have these joys in full possession."

> night has lost
> its yellow light
> in the white constellation
> known as Amor Oculae

The indecisive man without yellow shirt is sitting on the bed holding his head in his hands.

The complications of other people's propensities sometimes simplify our own. There is something in the nature of tourism, that form of last exploration, which makes this true.

Lying beside Now-No-Yellow-Shirt, whom we had pleased immensely and temporarily without telling him anything about our travel plans, we enjoyed the difference between time and place, and time and time, and place and place, while waiting for him to fall asleep. When he did, we departed, pleasantly regretting it.

> greeting vehicle
> oh halted life
> wheeling immensely
> our clothes are full
> love rusts infinity
> without disgust

Like many a returning traveler, we are in the presence of things to come to terms with as we float back to a yet more familiar sky. "Things" is that ordinary word meaning lost to present knowledge. And floating is a mode of returning, which is determined by a

sense of loss, or conversely and identically, by a sensation of having
occupied a space in the proximity of a retrievable object. Just as if
one were trying to explain oneself to a stranger. Thus, as figures,
traveling and returning meet.

pressure in sameness
logos
a sublime—without

our body
is perfectly posed
when violence is the subject

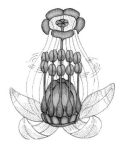

MAY 12

Dear Lyn,

It seems to me that this may be the right moment to start a correspondence; I think we need to take a break from accumulating fragments. The difficult aspects of sex or sexuality may have to do with the way the fragmented form has evolved to this point. In addition to our eagerness to work in the most obvious genre that traveling used to suggest, the letter, a correspondence, might give us more thoughts about the fragmentation that thus far has constituted our excursion. Might I consider this insert erotic?

But it is odd, funny to be writing to you about our work-in-progress as a part of the work itself.

In one of our recent conversations you mentioned your resistance to violence in Bataille and to "dark sex," and this I think creates a fruitful tension between us: we have to negotiate our individual experiences and our thinking about, or feelings for, the "erotic" in order to write anything together at all. Some of the tension is explicit, even judgmental, and other aspects of it go unstated; in a sense they remain eroticized.

We have arrived at a site where anxiety over sexuality is connected to forms of non-erotic, political violence within the frame of our pleasure-laden writing. Yet, the writing's disposition toward pleasure does not disappear when the Haitian elections are referred to, but the language changes key. The word "Macoute" is eroticized in our use of it, because part of the "landscape" of the writing is "sound" and the sound of the word exceeds its social meaning—or acts as an indication of another kind of meaning in which terror and sexuality entwine in fantasy. Yet the morose affect of "Macoute" in the poem is a sign, or symptom, of both protest and disappointment in what seems to be a hopeless situation—the invisible power operating outside the narratives of the news. How often are the U.S. interests in controlling such nations as Haiti made apparent to us through the media?

In bits of the material leading up to this correspondence, I have been attempting to show, rather than to explain, the imagination's vulnerability to and working with the associations between mediated images, narratives, documentary, cultural knowledge, and fantasy.

Here fantasy, as gendered, is related to the feminine projection of power onto men—through an autobiographical lens. When I was around twelve, I saw a news documentary on Papa Doc, the Haitian Dictator. He and his "Macoute" thugs were "scary guys." In the girl's mind it is easy for the scary guy to become associated with scary adult male sexual power/desire. Power and desire of the other are sites of projection. Here "the other" is also an ethnic other; his opposite would be those Haitians who oppose and/or are suppressed by the power of the Macoute. How does this information impress itself on the mind of a twelve-year-old white girl in California?

As an adult, I have read about the history of the Haitian political struggle as well as about its culture with great interest. But in what capacity could or would I go to Haiti? Not as a tourist.

Yet the passages related to Haiti in *The Wide Road* initiate a tour (this sounds frighteningly militaristic); what I have done is read and respond to an American newspaper's representation of current events, absorbing these into the erotic undertow of our imagination.

Right now I am imagining a bright flashlight shining on a body, my own or anybody's; the body in this frame becomes "just a naked body"—the same as, or close to, a dead body. Then I think: expose, exposition. Then: detective, police novel, and genre.

Oddly, I just now recall that there is an actual experience related to the image of the body exposed with a flashlight. I was in a building occupied by anarchists in Paris, sleeping next to a young man. The police came to arrest us for illegally sleeping in the building. One of the police, a white person of about my age, turned his light on me while I dressed. I kept telling myself "just put on your clothes, you're just a body to him. It doesn't matter, I'm just a body." By convincing myself that what was happening didn't matter and that I was only matter, I was removing myself from the place where I could be violated or threatened. But the distant feeling I communicated, by having removed myself from my physical body, brought out the sadism in the cop, who then attempted to belittle me for sleeping with "Chinois." He informed me that my transgression would make my babies dirty. It was this comment that terrified me; it was then that I became fearful of not knowing what would happen next. If he could say anything, perhaps he felt that he could do anything too.

What do you make of these thoughts that link violence, sexuality, fantasy, and autobiography?

Love, Carla

Dear Carla,

Here is a nonviolent scenario: A bends to B, B bends to A—both are wielding power and both are submitting to it in a game of pleasure, A or B on top, B or A wiggling and waving. But power at play with pleasure is not violence: "I silence your moaning with violins."

I'm side-stepping your question—but not the challenge it entails. I'm giving myself time to think, to fantasize, to range through my own associations. We live in an aftermath condition—or aftermath is the condition in which what you are calling our fragments (the intentionally under-explicated bits of some implicitly vaster story, only semi-contextualized expository asides, and the very asidedness of our attention and the dubious duplicity of our personage) become, at least for me, a topography. At one point in the writing, I crafted a gnomic phrase; it was some meta-comment like "we will not know where we will go." It deserved the rejection / deletion that it received. But it did point to a tension between power and play, intention and open inadvertency, willfulness and willlessness that pulls at this extended foray into erotic adventure and pastoral contemplation; the work has multiple centers of gravity. Your question demands an understanding of the resulting topography; I'm on the verge of asserting the undesirability of that.

Power at play with pleasure is not violence: "I silence your moaning with violins."

The situation becomes ominous when *pleasure* is at play with *power*.

Or am I getting too metaphysical? I think so. A metaphysical conceit is a poor substitute for the linkages that constitute mattering.

"My dear, you are a genius in a pink and black harlequin suit."

"My dear, take my high-powered flashlight."

Various caricatures come forward into the light: there is the squeamish cowpoke with a quirt, the sentimental general with a lapdog, the revolting torturer with perfect teeth, the 8-year old girl in the dark. The girl is tossing in ersatz feverishness, coddling a pretend broken arm, indulging in a fantasy of hospitalization or imprisonment where passivity is mandatory, culpability impossible: whatever pleasures she will experience won't be her fault and her endurance will be heroic. I can remember much of this; it came to me when I learned of the Holocaust. The sentimental general presses the prongs of a red hot fork into the paws of his lapdog. That happened in the aftermath of monotheism, the aftermath of the Inquisition, the aftermath of colonialism.

Invention directed toward the repression of invention as well as the repression of alterity has provided "dark sex" with some disturbing instruments and eroticism with disturbing instrumentality. Cruelty, the use (inevitably eroticized) of torture as an instrument of power, the violence to optimism that even milder misuses of power produce, the defamation of the very notion of power so that creative uses of power are perceived as threatening, even monstrous—our gender, fantasy-life, the soil underlying concrete highways and crushed by cars, etc., have been devastated by these.

Submission, even to violence, does have its place in the realm of the erotic, but the violence in the sex is not necessarily inflicted violence; it can also be violence that is very precisely, even meticulously, withheld, as the prolongation of an otherness that occurs only in and as sex.

The sound "Macoute" is, as you say, eroticized in our use of it, and I don't think glibly. Among other things, we are pointing to the pleasurability of round and percussive sound; the play of lips and teeth and tongue involved in making it; the aesthetic triumph of referent over reference; the danger inherent in the drift of signifiers out of context.

But, Dear Carla, a letter should *open* with the setting of a scene. It should show the letter-writer in her scene so as to produce an inviting passage through which the writer brings the reader in. This may be considered erotic. Dear Carla, I have just closed the windows. Outside, the wind is blowing and I can see the branches of the neighborhood trees leaping and shaking, though whether they are trying to get into or get out of the wind and sunlight it's impossible to say. Now that I'm paying attention to the scene, I notice that I'm not sitting up straight. I should do so. I'm wearing black socks, my favorite black pants, an old and comfortable long-sleeved purple thermal shirt, and I've wrapped a blue and white long scarf around my neck.

There is a calculator on the desk along with assorted papers, and Bataille's *The Impossible.* Opening it at random, as a bibliomancer might, I come upon this phrase: "his guiding concept." For me, *The Wide Road* has multiple guiding concepts, and apart from those that might be more obvious, compassion and animal exhaustion (death) are among them.

People are still fighting to be people; why do they hold animals in contempt?

Love, Lyn

Dear Lyn,

Would one be an exhausted animal if one felt that the proper thing to do is thank the mountain when one uses its resources to build a wall? Is one brought to the edge of animal exhaustion not only because of the limits of a lifespan but because one fears the time it would take to live with a different relationship to mountains and oceans? Is the fear of time, or taking the time to make a world in which people can live, actually the fear of not being able to accomplish this before death—the fear of life-span and of failure?

Do you think of people as animals? I ask this question of you now, without quite knowing what it is I'm asking. It is a dated question, stemming from a time in which the human was set apart from the animal first within religious and then within secular culture. Humans thought of themselves as special beings, superior to all living things, because they knew that they were either immortal or mortal. We still think this way, don't we? Even if the values we have constructed through this belief have reached the dead-end to their claims over nature. We think (or do I mean behave?) at the site of a dead-end, even as we suspect or know its falsity.

Does this dead-end have anything to do with Freud's "death drive," a revised version of which seems to be currently in high throttle? As we have been discussing on our recent companionable walks, some species, but possibly not ours, will survive the massive destruction currently underway, which may or may not be precisely linked to this concept.

If animals did hold us in contempt then we are animals and they are people, and vice versa. "Held in contempt" is a juridical term. Would it please the psyche to be put on trial by creatures? Would this relieve one from terrible guilt? I can imagine the cardinals in my backyard finding me guilty in a toad's court. But if they find me guilty, what will they do? Perhaps the penalty will be that they will refuse to be in the same world as me: and this has already happened, without the trial.

I am looking at the reproduction of a photograph of an 18th century drawing of two children who share the same hair.[1] By necessity, they are standing so close together that it is difficult to discern if they are joined in any other part of the body. In any case, they are not facing the same direction: one child offers the viewer a profile and the other a semi-frontal view: they are rendered as a

---

1    George Bataille, *Documents*, ed. Bernard Noël (Mercure de France, 1968), 114

specimen. Perceiving them in this way is uncomfortable, at least to me. My description of them is a sign of an ambivalent impulse: I want to describe what I see as a way of pointing to something that is not what I see. Additionally I can't tell you if what I don't see is predominately the limitation of my own perceptions or the limitation of the photograph itself.

Though one of the children does not seem to be looking up, her head, along with her outstretched arms, gestures upward. The other child, in an oppositional pose, gestures toward the ground. Do these specimens invoke an allegory that exceeds the evidence of the document? Because the upward positioned child appears taller than the downward facing child, it seems that the hair joining them is forcing them to exist in a limiting symbolic relation to one another. Yet one can imagine that the smaller child might have the physical leeway to stand in a higher spot with some maneuvering and change its position, and therefore its symbolic, or token, value, relative to its twin.

The hair connecting them is beautiful, a perfectly groomed fluid thing: water-nature and culture combine in this faux clinical study. Yet the evidence shows that the most obvious condition of the children is that flow in movement is restricted by an aberration. Can I read this as an allegory of mimesis?

At the feet of one child is a clump of rocks and scanty vegetation and at the feet of the other is a plant that approximates the size and shape of the rock: this reminds me of weeds mimicking the other growth around them in order to trick the weed picker. Is the allegory I am conjuring, or hinting at, an illusionist trick strategically produced through the style of the document?

I could describe the drawing in more detail, focusing on the children's postures and the representation of their facial features, but what interests me more than the specific differences and similarities between them is the odd sense that the more I look at the "deviants" the more I see distinctions, individuality, and separateness: the generic documentary presentation of the reproduction does not completely reduce the twinned and joined figures to "type" even as type of aberration. Furthermore, this document elicits in me a feeling of tension between "category" and "particular" as co-existing in a crisis. And this crisis is signaled in a feeling, that of repulsion. Science or philosophical distance cannot stave off this sensation. Is the *feeling* of repulsion toward the deviant an intended effect? Does the document with its overlay of clinical evidence ironically dismantle its distancing function through some kind of interstitial event of subject, subjectivation, and document, which is ironically presented as "a thing"? What is objectified then are not the represented children but the document itself? And the feeling of being repulsed is a feeling about the document as a thing?

In reviewing my responses, I return to my observations about the non-human forms, rock and plant, that appear as approximations of each other: distinct type blurs into sameness. This viewer joins or brings closer together what is categorically separate in her reading of the photograph. Desire to make sense of evidence has arrived at a place where the fascination with separation and sameness, as an asymmetrical pairing, are reflected in the objectification of deviation. This strangeness, or strained relation, between separate and same reminds me of our questions about animals.

Love, Carla

P.S. At this moment we are looking at unqualified ecstasy.

a mother's tongue
fixed to a man's throat
when his mouth opened

And the clinical scrutiny changes to views of a stage where an antiquated heroine of the early 20th century sings, "To kings and thieves add mothers"—as did Brecht. A newspaper reporter wrote later, "It was rather like a shower of fireworks, but so bewildering and so dazzlingly bright that it blinded the watchers." But the women in the back, nursing their babies, did not notice much of this.

We had been "hiding out" in an office building where we had been given some temporary work, so after the show we returned there with our book on the French Revolution, which, in our late night fatigue, we used as a pillow. It may be that the women I refer to above were propping up our head.

P.P.S. Bataille writes, "This sickness [deviation] is obscurely bound to an intense seduction." I leave this in the fractured arena of those of one head and two minds.

Dear Carla,

I raise my head and look out the window; sunlight glinting off the side of a passing car captures my attention. That is not an animal. The attention of vegetarian-browsing animals is probably first drawn to things that don't pass by (clumps of grass, a thistle's flower-head, etc.), whereas carnivorous-predatory animals are on the lookout for moving things, even though some are inedible (like the passing car). There are hairy-furry animals, and feathered ones, also scaly, and naked ones, and shiny-shelled ones (beetles, for example) as well as dull-shelled ones (e.g., crabs). There's a bee crawling along the bottom edge of the window and it puts me in mind of spiders and caterpillars, which in turn bring me back to the hairy-furry category. Newts and salamanders are naked. Humans are hairy-furry plus naked, same and separate from amphibians and the canine-feline-bovine-equine-ungulate animals that humans like to tame, pet, train, work, ride, gaze into the eyes of, etc., the ones humans generally feel the greatest affinity with. Sometimes in crowds I have an overwhelming impulse to stroke people's skin or hair, in exactly the way I would like to touch a giraffe's neck or an ostrich's wing—out of sentient curiosity.

In my last letter I continued with the notion of "mattering" that you raised in your first letter—where "matter" refers to literal materializing and to significance, importance, something worth caring about (emotionally, intellectually, ethically, amorously, etc.). The linkages you imagine when you speak of one's thanking a mountain for the use one makes of it—or, as I would hope one might, thanking it simply for being there, for making an appearance (as the white-tailed kites we saw together above a coastal meadow did, to our mutual delight)—I want to forge and continuously feel such linkages. To live in a disenchanted world is to live at a dead-end. In *The Wide Road* "we" finds enchantments. The work may be an allegory about artists and the role of art-making. It is certainly a work about creative sexuality, and about sportive mindful animality.

Yes, I think of humans as animals, although, being (I'm pretty sure) temperamentally incapable of what we would call a strictly animal existence (dedicated exclusively to the necessities of personal and species survival—the cycle of feeding, sheltering, and reproducing), I have to admit that I feel in some ways superior to (other) animals. But is it really the case that only human animals are capable of setting self-interest aside in favor of other principles? Are there not instances of dogs racing into a burning building to save a human? The mother killdeer draws the predator away from her eggs or chicks by hopping close to it, dragging one wing.

She may know just how close she can get to the predator while preserving her safety, but surely there's a risk involved. The ethical sphere, which philosophy in the Kantian tradition considers to be peculiar to humans, may not be. Ethical thought may be peculiarly human, but ethical actions may not be sheerly ethical. The question remains, however, just how ethical an action is if it takes place without thought? No. The question is, must we, in our rejection of sentimentality, really believe that animals don't have thoughts?

Many of our human thoughtful calculations and strategies and ploys, which we rationalize so intricately and so philosophically (abstractly), may be no more complicated than the killdeer's pretending to be wounded—her so-called "instinct."

When I was young I was less conscious of my animal nature than I am now. Now I often notice myself as an animal, but that only means that I am increasingly aware of my physical body, which is either "me" or "mine"—I'm not sure which. One's physical body, in itself, can be rendered astoundingly alien when sufficiently considered. I have at hand (looking at my hand) the amazing possibility of being intimate with my own otherness, which is an animal.

It is seductive to think that this particular experience—but it may not be experience but, rather, yearning—this yearning for intimacy with one's own otherness, and the casting of that into the soul-eyes of an animal (which is to say into an unfathomable speechless mortal expressivity)—it is seductive to think that this animal-wish allows us to approach the death toward which the death wish drives us.

The "death drive" (as you term it, but I've also seen Freud's term rendered into English as the "death wish," and I like that better, for reasons you'll see in what I'm about to say)—so, the death wish desires, like a head with two minds, two different deaths— that of the other, and that of oneself. It simultaneously activates one's longing for autonomy and superiority (which would be accomplished by killing the other) and one's longing for oceanic belonging that is inherent to eternal indivisibility (which would be accomplished by dying).

Both, in a vicious and sick way, are being enacted in the planetary climatological catastrophe that's currently underway and in spreading wars in their various manifestations. Some are local, some more widely regional, some are being carried out on a nearly continental scale, all are global in effect and they seem increasingly to be not only related to but produced by climate disaster. Both are also, and far better, enacted in the little death of orgasm, when one so voluptuously merges into not-one—into no-one and more-than-one—the little deaths that occur as "we" cuts the swathe we call the wide road.

> eating but ordinary sleepers
> hurry fragrantly—flagrantly
> the warm sun is soaked, locked, flopping
> the plank is popping

My dog Flash looked a lot like my mother. There was something about the animal skin and fur around Flash's lips and eyes that, in their vulnerability and difference, and dependable accessibility to my gaze, made me think of my mother. Maybe all that means is that if one stares at anything long enough and thinks one owns it, it will eventually resemble one's mother.

We are born with a death wish. Or we develop one. Either way, the mother is a factor here. I do not want to be (like) my mother.

Love, Lyn

Dear Lyn,

> when the clouds pass over
> the plank becomes
> a narrative
>
> we want to soak
> and explode
>
> our present object's
> faces and our private sight

You might remember this poem in a longer version, one that masked its violence, a little.  But before I comment more on this baffling emission, I want to let you know that I very much enjoyed your last letter. I appreciate the kindness and generosity of your tone as well as the way you refresh our conversation by staying with the subject. Your letter addresses my previous letter while sustaining the "free spirit" of letter writing. And I so enjoy the evident pleasure you take in piling in *details*, which are received by this reader as welcome *events*.

Today, I am writing you mulling over the strange poem above—and letting this lead me, somewhere. It is not particularly a lucid thing and was written in a frustrated, or worse, angry, mood.

Like an angry person, the poem exhibits an impulse to create and to destroy something all at once. In it are tumultuous associations that appear to suggest an erotic obliteration of the object. The most violent part of the poem is the expressed wish to both soak and explode the face of "our" object. Please excuse me for using the plural—but for me this is a meaningful part of our fiction, which here displaces private emotion onto the scene of our collaboration.

And yet in further considering what I have just written to you, I find in this language a little revelation about our book. Let us say that social ideology that represses sexuality and/or channels it in instrumental narrative is the face of our object. And that the "private sight," which we wish to explode is that thing that never signifies in the face of the object. The desire is to explode the private sight such that it becomes apparent and, in a sense, dispersed, or incoherent. Let us say that there is a need for this incoherence—so that the plank does not become a narrative that is redundantly reproduced. "We" is not walking the plank but we are preparing a future object, including this book.

In choosing in my last letter to use the term "death drive" that you then took up, or qualified, as "death wish," I was emphasizing the energetic, instinctual, or inaccessible force that motivates behavior. I want to converse with you just a bit more about "wish" and "drive," with only *some* allegiance to Freud and the psychoanalytic tradition, as I am interested in the tension between these two words as indicative of a paradox within our work and not in attempting, so much, to rehearse a theory.

"Wish" indicates subjectivity and "drive" does not. Let me first say something about "wish." A pleasurable utopian impulse motivates our construal of an erotic adventure. The wish, as I identify it here, and which inflects Ernst Bloch's construct of hope, is akin to an erotic feeling, one that we can channel or direct in writing. It is a writing that hinges on a radical contingency of continuity and discontinuity. Neither continuity nor discontinuity are exclusively a result of "wish" or "drive" in our project, yet wishful desire does play an important part in our multi-directional narrative and its contingent non-narrations.

The wish is also contingent upon the self-negating instinctual drive, which appears as some kind of force over which a wishful Eros, or subjectivity, has no impact. (Hello, Freud!)

Yet there exist spaces for the negation of this drive, and one of these is the space of "play." Play is a medium in which the drive is encountered without significant threat to the subject.

But within the field of play, the drive is shattered and figured. It is transformed into objects with plastic qualities. Thus the fragmentation of the writing is also a feature of psychic shattering on the site of a destructive condition. I suppose that what I am saying in my own melancholy way is that, for myself, this shattering, which ultimately exceeds the effects of play, is necessary.

I am going to end here with a scene from daily life, despite its lack of continuity with the more obvious concerns of this letter:

I would never deny that I can get choked up at the sight of a beautiful human being. Yesterday, a young mother was holding her child, facing her friend whose back was turned to me. The mother said to the child as she pointed teasingly at her friend, "Now isn't that the ugliest thing you've ever seen?" "She's a flower," said the little girl. The friend was laughing and so was I. She heard me and turned to look at me; and there was "the flower." She was large, with sloping shoulders and curving neck (totally the opposite of Bataille's stereotypical representation of the beautiful woman—he says that beautiful women are slender because they least resemble animals).

Later the beautiful friend was sitting sort of lumpishly on a concrete slab of the park's play structure, watching the mother and the little girl climb around. No matter how "bad" her posture and unconscious she was of her looks, her beauty would not go away. This account has something to do with the anger I discharged in writing the poem.

Love, Carla

Dear Carla,

Thank you for your totally wonderful letter. I've read it now several times, delighting in (and, I should add, learning from) the pairings that emerge from the ideas you are developing. The more I think about what I'm calling pairings, the more complex and suggestive they become. The terms appear always in incomplete (impossible) opposition, as elements incapable of similarity and incapable of separating from each other. Perhaps inevitably, given the doubling we've set in motion at so many levels in *The Wide Road*, we've a proclivity for heuristic bifurcations. Doubling is the subjective premise, or subjective stance, with which we negotiate fragmenting encounters; doubling is also one of its principal activities—indeed one of its principles.

"Doubling"—the notion as I'm trying to develop it here—isn't synonymous with "splitting" or "bifurcating" or even "twinning." You demonstrate that in your meditation on the drawing of the hair-bound pair of girls. Doubling is wishful. The conditions we are generating are dialectical ones of shifting relations and proliferating sense-objects; there are more and more things to experience, even in a single event. To "double" (and I'm going to drop this term in a moment—and I can bet you'll say "good riddance") is also to produce elements for linkage. We seem to be particularly given to unlikely linkages, to exciting mismatches, to the creative (playful, powerful, funny, mournful) co-existence of live incommensurabilities. Clouds pass over and a plank becomes a narrative—an unlikely event erupting (because of anger?) from an unlikely logic—and therein we sense a situation, the site of a crisis.

What a strange pastoral landscape our picaresque buddy-being wanders in.

You say you were angry when you wrote that "we want to soak / and explode." "We" had perceived a threat (or maybe a bevy of threats) to which the best response was the disruptive orgasmic defense. It's a potent defense against coercive schematization—doubling to the zillionth power.

Passing clouds ugly, fictive private lumpishness, plank beauty, slender soaking, face explosion: "she's a flower." Drive schematization is made ludicrous by sentient soaking-explosive doubling.

Writing this letter to you is fun.

Paul Valéry says (in *The Analects*), "Two dangers never cease threatening the world: order and disorder."

Is it possible that the drawing of the two girls sharing hair is an allegorical portrait? And that your meditation on aberrance as repulsion-deviance curiosity (or curiosity as deviant-repulsion aberrance) interprets that allegory?

Sorry—I know I'm projecting my own turgid set of concepts onto your meditation. But I do think that one impulse informing our writing in *The Wide Road* is a search for knotty (and sometimes naughty?) entailments. We are learning eros—for example, the logic of car engines, of babies in a park, of insults, ballot propositions, coat pockets, the aftertaste of certain foods, the postal system, soft-core war reporting, fantasies that are lodged in the world as a beautiful lumpishness that won't go away, the affective force of a word like "fuck."

Let's say we are... we are on a boat in the Indian Ocean. We are pregnant—no—we are willing to be. The erotic could be linked to reproduction. We are optimistically instinctual and animal; we are vivacious and pleasurably vulnerable. We know exactly where our passport is, we have anticipated a change of currency and we've already converted some of our pesos (euros/drachmas/

rubles/dollars) into the next local *valuta*. Our underwear is strung across a porthole in the sun to dry, and there is plenty of shampoo remaining in the bottle. Now we'd like a bit of goat cheese and a cracker—one can never learn too much eros. We'll get a job. We want our life wish to signify.

We—I mean, "we"—finds it stupid not to fuck. Such stupidity would be an abnegation of our wishfulness. I am not familiar with the clinical drawing you described in your June 10 letter, although I've seen what I imagine to be similar evidentiary documents—drawings and also photographs of "aberrant types," "freaks," etc. The uses to which the documents might be put includes the prevention of their subjects fucking. Normative ideology disallows the reproduction of aberration. Susan Schweik, in *The Ugly Laws: Disability in Public*, has written extensively on laws enacted to keep the disabled (described as "monstrous" and "ugly" and "an offense," etc.) out of sight. It was against the law for them to be seen in public. "Now isn't that the ugliest thing you've ever seen?" Normative ideology wants to preclude the aberration from daily life. "She's a flower," said the little girl. She may very well have been angry.

Love, Lyn

epistolary chance reprise
recapitulation's tease
in last night's dream
of a vernal penis

Last night's dream of a vernal (green) penis might be taken as a prediction of rain and the end of winter. We don't know. Our vagina is now approaching but it is still far away.

There's so much to do.

We cannot find ourself asleep on our side, only awake there, taken from the receptive continuity of a dream—sex with someone and solicitude for a younger man—this is a dream about birdwatching—and we get out of bed, pushing up from the pillow with the right arm, the skin of our arm still impressed with the weight of our having slept, both feet on the floor—no rug just there, only wooden slats about two inches wide and decoratively mismatched. We are round.

The room is still blind.

We brush our teeth—selecting our toothbrush is automatic—it isn't property but person.

The mouth held open, the green toothbrush reading the teeth from left to right.

The activities of the Marquis de Sade either exceed or close over the boundaries of our person. We appeal to our daily life, which is persistently abnormal but adorable (we are slaves to it), to provide us with the authority of our anti-authority—a mule is to a carpenter what a pine nut is to breakfast.

It is still morning. From another room we hear a man zipping his pants. We see a big dog setting the pace for a woman out walking it, while the sound of a police helicopter hangs overhead, supposing that some crime can be concluded. If *subliminal* means meaning that's hidden, can we say *surliminal* to speak of meaning exposed?

In the kitchen, where the floor meets the wall, crumbs accumulate—they get greasy—we are irritated, overwrought. We can't throw anything away.

Paradise is a damaged situation.

We think—we write: We eroticize our earthly situations and conditions and likewise they eroticize us. So we've been both the subject and the object of desire and the origin and recipient of pleasure on many occasions.

But daily life is a very ambivalent agent of desire—perhaps that's what makes it so compelling as an agent of writing. The oscillation between interior and exterior of what seem to be the contents of our experiences makes our daily life simultaneously expressive of Us and of Not-Us.

We are thinking about both mitigated and unmitigated sex.

> without hiding
> we are hidden
> though monuments
> explode an interior

"A word is the purest and most sensitive medium of social intercourse," we bark. Like selves equated to distant beings, our shadows exchange fists in the parking lot. A poised fist is not sexual in its potential to select a surface, but "I," a word our shadows have wandered away from, unnerves a passerby.

In its own uplifting splash, the "I" continues its rap, intervenes with the fist, counts out, while we, diffuse and borrowed, walk into the bank building and undress a pot that houses a more permanent resident, a nicely dwarfed palm, one of many nicely dwarfed palms manicured in rows next to the rows of elevators.

The elevators slide through the interior of the building while we write a letter to Mono. Dear Mono. Command. Command. If there is no obedience there is no privacy. After signing the letter

> we are caught
>
> making love
>
> in the pot

"Are you talking to yourself as you do that?" asks the woman. She has come into the corridor near the elevator shafts with a companion, a man. We drop the soft palm frond with which we had engaged in almost unbearable tickling. We are still muzzy with desire. Though on the one hand the arrival of this couple in the corridor might offer us a new pleasure, that of being seen, they have in fact interrupted our love-making. It is difficult, in any case, to turn our attention to her question enough to understand it. What is she really asking us?

"Do you engage in what the poet from the woods calls subvocalization?" asks the man. "Like when you read a book of poetry and sort of hear the words in your head even though you aren't intentionally sounding them out?"

"Yes, do you?" asks the woman. "With something that has a story in it, too, or contains a fragment of a narrative. Like, when *I'm* having sex, it's like I'm having a story. I hear things like, 'She spread her legs as he softly ran his tongue across her vagina.'"

"The third person!" we exclaimed.

> the voice is blue
> her kiss shines
> this is wonderful
> and window

The differences between sound and sight are semantically inessential—at least this seems to be true of literary experience. But the third person was asking about sound and the senses in an extra-literary experience, involving the tender but erect tip of a palm frond, the tongue, the genitals, ourself, and the third person in a corridor—all of which we took to a room, where the curtains were still drawn across the window.

Sometimes we accept the enormous situation of the subject-object, wherein we exhibit (but we could say *embrace*) some of our capacities.

praises

praises

porosity

Palaver eros. Token eros. Palaver eros. Token eros. We chant to ourself crossing our twelve limbs with our new friend, the third person, in her room. This is private to he who can neither see nor hear us on the other side of the door but public to you who are always up to the minute on our every change of tune and crossing. We use our chant, token eros, palaver eros, token eros, palaver eros as protection from The Whimsical Male Sexual Appetite (you can find this term in our favorite whodunit, Chapter 15). The Whimsical Male Sexual Appetite, as anybody probably already knows, often manifests itself in the guise of intellectual curiosity, which peaks quickly before we've even had a chance to take off our party masks and untie our shoelaces. His curiosity is never satisfied and our answer remains behind our party masks. We have ways around the WMSA and one of those ways is our little chant, which defends us well enough, yes yes, as we lock arms and legs in sitting squatting lying and standing positions. This is a nasty digression.

"Please feel free to question us on our side of the keyhole," we say to the man on the other side of the door, "but first you must get through it."

> it prods the air
> with tiny amps
> to baffle the instrument

(While we wait for him to work or slither or prod or whisper or wish his way through, let us take you on a little journey out onto the street where we pass first a girl walking like a confetti boy whirling on a skateboard in a slump with her ears plugged into the radio. And we say she is not us. While we say this a radio from a passing car says in a song, "I am glad I'm not Bob Dylan and Bob Dylan is glad he's not me." But before we can ask ourself why this might be so, an Egyptian woman passes us in sandals. It's the dead of winter, the trees bare, the air chill, and her feet walk on invisible pillows. But how do we know she's Egyptian? It's what the Eastern European woman with the thick skin, which she prizes above all her other magnificent physical attributes, told us in the sauna; we believed the storyteller. And we say as a lumbering man passes by, she is not us, or he. The more we say she is not us or he is not us the more a disagreeable sensation grows in us: of being childless with children, of being companionless with friends, of being loveless with lovers, of our bodies flooded with desire but repulsed by all possible objects of desire. We see a girl wrap her arm around her mother and we feel sickened by biology.)

Inside, where time is an inch of crushed clouds, where sponges select their cosmogony, where deltas spawn sage pudding, where an upheaval of leaves fumbles the senses, we dictate porosity.

>     patched prose
>     turns to holes

Or was it holes turning to prose?

Finally, the man surges through the keyhole—oily and bruised (but fit enough)—onto our bosom so we can get a few pinches of wisdom from his public open palm. It, the palm, strokes our mask, swelling with story, the inventor of privacy.

>     our bodies quiver
>     with angelic resolve

He sipped a hot drink, we removed our mask. It was the old story, the revolutionary one. In fact, at any given moment, a woman knows exactly what she wants.

"But you too," we said to the third person as the man ran his tongue along the rim of the warm cup around which he'd curled both his hands, "you too" (the man was or wasn't listening, but we couldn't have been more interesting)—"you too probably remember that time in late girlhood, that period of wiggling and lethargy, when you thought that the pressure within—the swelling inside your skull—was from something you didn't know. We know that we thought then that ignorance (increasing daily, since every experience added to it) was our Freudian destiny, part of the great triad of determinisms" (the man finished his drink and put down the cup), "along with the Darwinian one that shaped your inadvertent and obsequious cruelty while giving you a desire for the first person, and the Marxian one" (the man moved as if to stand up, but with every hand we pushed him back down and held him there) "that said you'd go down in history."

"Both Darwin and Freud say you'd go down for men," the man said.


"Palaver eros," we answered. "Go to bed."

It was a Monday of voluptuous stammerings, then a Tuesday without resolve.

a fantastic privacy often manifest

in us it is excited


One can see that from a certain point of view, a woman when it comes to sex is always on the outside.


But do you think that's what it's like to be a cup?


To what *that* are we referring, to what *what*, to what *it*?


There is a languid eros within a language eros.


As we'd lain, subject to the palm frond, subject-object to an eternal scene, outside the snow—now tinted red and blue by the setting sun and the scattered streetlights—was drifting, the sidewalks had turned icy, a slush was forming on the city's little river, and we dressed to go down to the narrow park, across which we would walk to the shops. The very young Latvian was tender as we took his arm, covering our bare fingers in the wool of his heavy coat. "When I was a very small child," he said, hunching his shoulders to lift the collar of his coat higher around his neck, "so little that I couldn't reach to hold onto anything to keep from falling in the bus, it was my greatest pleasure in life to wait in the morning for a very crowded bus, and then to enter it and find a place where many large women were riding crowded together in the aisle, and squeeze myself between them, against their warm coats and bodies—and then I would slowly fall asleep."

What is it that brings these women to city parks in the cold to feed the ducks? We ourself love to feed ducks. More and more of them coming to what we offer. Throwing the bread, in our privacy we forget everything. We can never satisfy them.

neither willing
nor unwilling
no departure
in another hour

Dear Reader, with our thick skin and slump and our feet walking on invisible pillows, we recreate the previous episode for our Eastern European friend while in the sauna. I hope you will forgive our inconsistency, as well as repetitiveness; please understand that a story, when held up as an object for another's perusal, has a prismatic effect. Or one might say "psychoanalytically" that a story is dependent upon who one is speaking to to come into being. It differs from receptor to receptor in the telling of it. The child who must explain her flat bicycle tire to a father who only wants yes and no answers has a completely different method of persuasion

than the child who is required to give a full explanation, even if
this be the same child in different contexts. Therefore, the subject
is multiple.

Therefore, the man said:
(we told the woman
in the heated room) a woman
knows what she wants.

We say he said
The rim of this cup
promises satisfaction
to the lips.

We say he said
The rim of this cup
arranges my hand around it
as a gift from mother.

Therefore (we tell the woman)
the man said:
The rim of this cup arranges
what women want they know.

Our friend of the sauna began to complain: but you or he, I can't tell which, left everything of interest out of the story! There is no content only poetry in that. I should tell you what it was like to be a boy-chaser in Zolt. That's a story. I can remember every stone on the street. The one that dislodged under my fierce bicycle.

In the alley next to the brilliant street I would hide and wait for someone perfect to pass. Passersby harassed me while I waited. You do-nothing, you know-nothing would hammer in my head daily. But when I found the perfect human being I'd pass their harassment of me onto him. It worked perfectly until he lost his glow. Since he was no longer perfect, I begged him to leave. Eventually another perfect person would pass....

Nowadays, I no longer have a bicycle that could dislodge a stone.

We felt so happy, there in the sauna, our languid eros meeting her language eros. Finally, we told her about the Latvian waiting for us. We hugged all around and bid farewell, keeping in mind the cautionary tale she had just recited, and at the same time secretly praising certain forms of repetition.

Between duck
and Latvian
who needs
perspective in
another hour?

Dear Reader, have we invited you in?

We are excessively worried about fat.

Your worries are redundant, but our lunch is not. It is progress. A transformation is enacted through repetition. A plate of peas (in a green cascade) is like a night in bed with a reader—well, as long as the reader hasn't taken up a book.

We will skip over all that we already know about self-destruction and the lover's look. Instead, naked with hospitality, in the midday winter sun, having prepared for everything—we can invite the reader in. The reader will help us shell peas.

Do you string your beans, and do you French them?

Does salt dry out your meat?

Do you peel the bottom ends of asparagus, and is an asparagus a spear of grass?

Weeping over our onion—really feeling a profound emotion—we became sentimental in the kitchen, naked, thinking about nature—we mean, long term continuing nonindividual nonhistorical human nature.

What's the population of this city? we called from the kitchen to the reader who was a local citizen.

650,000.

With overwhelming, melancholy detachment we considered the fact that every one of these 650,000 people has a belly and a chest.

What incredible vulnerability! we called from the kitchen.

What's that? he said.

The population is transient, we called back.

It's growing, he said.

We stepped to the kitchen door. It was true. It was growing. With tears streaming down our cheeks, with a dishtowel flung over our shoulder and across one breast, wearing not even a tiny apron, we said

> predictions are extra
> eggplants don't console
> we'll drink a little coffee
> desire is our goal

A really relentless cooperation should be possible out of all this steam. When we say desire in a context of coffee we mean, of course, clarity. When we say clarity in the context of girl lust, we mean we want to memorize.

The reader is lovable. He paid careful attention as we told him about the flat tire on our Schwinn girl's bicycle. We confessed to him that we'd been a boy-chaser in Zolt, where girls couldn't be boy-choosers. We were chasing a boy named Dumb Deedee and calling him names. A neighborhood girl named Leading Linda came out of her house—she'd been fingerprinting the kitchen garbage and was sure her mother was drinking up the brandy. Ben Clayton had just untied Ruthie and she was coming out of the cellar of his house in the cul-de-sac called Hillcrest Court. We were bicycling in circles just there, where our mother had said we could since no traffic went down the dead-end street, and we had to swerve to avoid Ruthie, just as Mrs. Clayton threw a bucket of roofing nails down at Dumb Deedee who was yowling like a randy cat on the sidewalk. We rode right over the roofing nails and the nails punctured the tire. We were a little girl and we fell like a yogi on all those nails—that was what initiated the first period of mysticism in that cul-de-sac.

lunching and sportive

given permission

"becoming" is not the opposite

of "the same thing"

Bulb: globular base of stem sending roots downwards and leaves etc. upwards; compressible globular rubber attachment for pneumatic operation of syringe, etc.; roundish swelling of any cylindrical organ, as of hair root or spinal cord; dilated part of glass tube, e.g. reservoir of thermometer; (glass container of) electric lamp

—*notebook entry dated 10/10*

Entering room with bundle of lilies. Still thinking. In bed, is there one or two? Laying the flowers on top of bundle under bedcovers. Will it stir? A thick hand emerges with a sleep spasm, ineffectively clutching at the edge of a blanket. The hand lies on top of the blanket. Round, padded, muscular, freckled. The thumb twitches.

Bending over the bed we insert a finger into the small cavern formed by the lightly curled hand. Is it the hand of one sleeper or the hand of one of two sleepers? Our bed seems fully occupied. But who is company? Is it peaceful in the bedroom? Will we frighten what sleeps if what sleeps wakes?

Now we sit in an overstuffed chair, with a bowl of freshly shelled peas between our legs. Downstairs, all our husbands are sleeping on cool mats after a long meal. They sleep among a scent of onions and cumin mingled with the sweet fragrance of speckled lilies.

We chew or suck on the peas one or two at a time, the little skins coming off in our mouth, held between the teeth while the tongue presses the soft green inner pea ball against the roof of the mouth. A breeze lifts the hem of our chemise.

A jerk of the covers on the bed reveals a fleshy and muscular, freckled mound of a male's ass, as large also as the width of our abundant bed. With confident grandeur, blunt plinthlike legs support this marvelous work of art.

The lilies

fall

dress

and address

the magician

with discretion


The wide feet are magnificently arched. He bends, over the white
width of belly. Small goosebumps feather his sumptuous arms and
shoulders. Our nipples harden.


Then

we

cover

him


Being animal and having less to do.

Or being "fluid" and having lots to do.

We are reaching across the rising, and then it curls back.

In the darkness in which his width glitters like untouched sand we
are allowed, inclined; he mumbles endearments like "honey" and
"amber" and "fraction" and "ash."

We don't want to speak. However now he asks us to describe; he urges us, he begs us. Then he presses us with real urgency: "Say it," he screams.

> we don't remember
> more
> our sleeps have gone
> to war

Each morning we leave our bed without sleep.

A warm breeze sucks at the curtains. In the dark we can see their motion but not their pattern as we lie again in our bed waiting for sleep.

For many nights sleep has failed to come.

There are only our hairs in the bed.

Sleep used to arrive dreamless and naked. Now there is only illusion, only dreams and heads.

Deep in the night millions of moths raising the dust off their wings flutter and crawl over the glossy black surface of the sky.

We, panting, turn in our room, thinking of sleep.

A milky blue steam rises to the surface of the sky.

Everything overlaps. All that is animate is abstract.

We are neither predisposed, nor disinclined, nor unfollowed.

The overlapping is all that lasts; the ghost of everything else occurs
in a flash.

We have a sexual dream, a blind sleeplessness.

We remember heat, the body of sleep, its breasts, its breath—but
sleep is at war, sleep only embraces antagonists, sleep roars.

       a dazzling dark
       joins on words
       where dreams remain
       they speed

We wondered at our oddness.

Sleep, we remember, kept to the right side of the bed and used only one pillow, while we like to use two. One of sleep's pillows was always thrown onto the floor.

Sleep often complained that it couldn't find its shoes. It worked all day in a truck, except when it stopped to eat eggs.

>     sex is compared
>     between darkness and pleasure
>
>     there is only a cricket?
>     who is our sleep?

In the morning it was we alone who loved. We analyzed it; we spoke it.

The toe was sucked into the Vagina Dentata. It tickled and came out just a little bloody. When we pulled the lips back to get a look at the machine, the teeth exposed gleamed, laughed, restored us to consciousness in the cave of silent validation. "Let me try it again this time with the lips pulled back," we said and inserted another big toe. The mouth only smiled invitingly, and the toe slipped out amiably enough but with a shadow of mild disappointment.

The shadow that sits
motherly behind
the rolling hilarity

This shadow recedes instantly we recognize the clump of undressed male standing root-like in the doorway. But first we put the dentata machine away. The man fears all that is physically funny, hungry, gigantic and self-contained in a woman; therefore, we sprinkle him with colored water and suck it up. We suck up the drops carelessly splashed on ourself and beg him to suck, lick, slurp, and bite it away. Immobile and dumbfounded, he lies there deep in brain waves with an enormous erection (of course!) that would have clanged against the metal of his armor had he had armor. We squeeze him between our legs.

What we could have been

Sleepy saints saving the sick in an idyllic mountain village where a sinister mirage has captured the hearts and imaginations of the population

Silent spies sneaking off to a sandy bank on the wet side of the island to restore ourself in a sanguine shelter cultivating our superiority with

our saucy and slick tongues together in the throes
of complete simplicity

Sodomists sado-masochists and everybody else
appearing at our cave entrance stylishly groomed
and bearing sausages once the news has leaked
around the island that the saints are sisters
spending the sappier part of each day playing each
other like saxes

Skindivers drenched in silt and scum from active
cave duty greeting the sadly surprised visitors
with brochures on syphilis and other sexually
transmittable diseases

Senatorial suckers sometimes shirkers driving up
suavely in their sooty suits suckers to discover that
we are merely screwballs

had we not been satisfied enough with all that had just passed.

And what was it that you wanted? the man asked us, after we had
smiled not from exhaustion but from vanity.

It's strange that an erection alone is never precise enough. We answered that it wasn't the erection by itself that we'd wanted— one would seldom, for example, refer to an erection as sweet—but rather all that had augmented it. What we always want is something all around.

For example we want an arrangement, preceded by preparation, and an erection can't be called a preparation. It is a result.

But preparation increases patience, and an erection, though it may feel impatient, is prepared, and so it may be one form of patience; arrangement is another.

And so we want preparation and arrangement.

Then time pokes space, but space also pokes time. And we adore the resulting space-time continuum. Fingers, ideas, a yielding to organization, the succulence of sea water, searching in the moist detail. Sometimes we feel that it's not our legs but time and space that spread when something enters.

> we are a candid sister
> you might wish for fifty
> we compel your sweetness
> to figure for its finger

It isn't leisurely to turn a man onto his back and climb over his erection. It's closer to oblivion—which is the opposite of vanity.

The man, meanwhile, had an indentation, and it wasn't independent; we were becoming fond of him.

> dentata, conductor, vagina, a village
> our teeth measure length
> his conductor seeks desire
> and our vagina
> is an engine of strength

There isn't anything we can't imitate. Sometimes this merely embarrasses us: "O dear, we did it again," we say remorsefully. "Okay," we are forced to admit, "we didn't read the book." But we begin again.

> our mother's paella
> ourself reprimanded
>
> instead of surreptitiously
> returning to the land
>
> solitude preparing
> a stone coming to its end

The northern California coast was dark and rocky. Fog rolled in against the cliffs like an airy higher ocean on which strange shadows and dreamed desires drifted.

We wanted to go out on a fishing boat and so we began to hang out on the docks, leaning ambiguously but industriously over the railing, smoking a cigarette and taking notes on the names of the boats and what they were bringing in. At night we maintained the same ambiguity when we drank in the waterfront bars, flirting with the fishing crews and awaiting a captain. Our hair was perpetually damp from the fog and spume that rose off the ocean and dripped off the fir trees and telephone lines. The damp made our curls thicker. In every way those were patient, humid days.

<blockquote>

our hum off a stiff horizon
a captain came with a can of nuts


his wet ship was in
its high fleas are fish
one flea reached the end of a pubic hair

</blockquote>

We thought the flea would belt us or scream, "You can't have him, he's mine!" We thought this because we'd been reading fables while watching TV in the fog. But then we realized for a second time that the flea was a fish, and its attraction to the crease between our legs was obvious.

> truly the legs are used
> in fog differently

we wrote on the side of the ship. The captain sent us the following response in a bottle filled with court bouillon:

> drink the fog differently
> sweeten the drifting leg's anchorage

We responded from the nether part of the ship:

> the drink drenches sheathed vegetation
> but what if greens need only a trickle?

Our robe fell off our shoulder while we awaited the next response. Any minute our fleshy legs smeared with court bouillon would turn to foam. What was keeping the captain? Anxiously we sat on our hand. A tickle crept down the inside of our thigh. It was the fish wiggling out of its hiding place. In surprise we moaned, "Oh." The next thing we knew an enormous breast had lodged itself in our mouth.

Simultaneously a hat fell on our foot. We could barely see it or feel anything except the court bouillon smeared all over us bulging with zeroes, all of them as soft as fawns' muzzles. Our head had been forced against the back of the bench by the mouthful of breast. We sucked voraciously and opened our legs as wide as we could to accommodate as many zeroes as possible. Our hand groped around on our thighs for the fish.

The captain laughed a feminine belly laugh. "You'll have to search my pockets for the fish." We were not timid. Our hands slipped into her tight little back pockets, which on the inside were full of holes. Little rounds of flesh were revealed to our fingertips. Cramped inside though they were, our fingers tore at the material, enlarging the holes until the inside of the pocket had been entirely ripped away. Our hands grabbed around each moon of ass. But our fingers, when they reached for that warm tunnel between moons, could not get there. We pulled them, cramping, out.

The retrieval of our hand from the dark caused, or seemed to have caused, the captain to jerk up and dislodge her breast from our mouth. We were a bit relieved, since it too was beginning to ache. "I need a break," she said and sat down, abruptly, next to us. Where just a minute before we had only a view of flesh and sky, we now had a view of a sailor standing next to a thick hose. But before we could remark on this, we realized that the captain had unbuttoned her pants and that she had placed her hand casually on her cunt mound. We were going crazy and jotted the following message on an old fig leaf we kept around for emergencies:

> We thought you'd be a man with
> a can of nuts drifting in the fog.
> Now the fog is fully fog. And we
> are fully anchored here. Your ship
> has joined us, too. But where
> is the can of nuts?

We read the note to her since she seemed unwilling to take it. As we spoke the word "nuts" she gave her clit a little pinch and gave way to what appeared to be an orgasm of great magnitude, which lifted her arching right up into the air and flipped her overboard. We ran to the side of the boat just in time to witness an enormous translucent fish tail disappear into the water.

We were then bent over the side of the boat looking a little sadly at the water. Its green fingers slapped the boat with a near lethargic desire. How were we to rid ourself of this over-population of zeroes pressing in at our thighs and filling up all our nether parts?

> let us lie
> under a waterfall

We walked inland for about fifteen minutes until we heard the gushing sound we had been hoping for. When we arrived at the site of the falls just over a shrubby hill, we found the sailor who had been watching us on deck, fully undressed, lying on a slippery rock right under the smallest of the waterfalls.

The water was striking him, directly but gently it seemed, and he had an enormous erection. We trembled with erotic emotion and let our robe slide away from our body. Water fell on our back and ass like a torrent of desiring hands and flapping fish. As we slid very slowly down on him, filling ourself with him, the zeroes began to pour sweetly out of us into the water, filling the water with our ohs.

Ecstasy was now rolling in a little stream and we lay at the edge of it. We tasted it with the tip of our tongue. The sailor moaned.

"You will never embarrass us," we said.

To dream means: We don't know what is happening to us.

Sleep always contains a little milk.

Heraclitus said, "Those who are awake have one and the same world in common; in sleep each one returns to his or her own world."

We snuggled with the sailor beside the water, watching the water perpetually divide and repeat. Occasionally we sipped—the water was always ready.

"What never leaves can never stay," the sailor said.

Soon the shadow of the evening sun was turning the water red, and the sailor put his pants back on.

> blind as milk
> but your hands full
> no seabirds can tell
> of our breasts as we blow

One night in a popular television cafe in the town of Rocky Welf we were sitting with a man who was drinking coffee. "The sea is not amorphous," he said, "I know this because I'm a bosun's mate. It is not a container, either. But if you know what you're doing you can fish with success. The sea, by the way," he added, "is not like music either."

"Our mother always said," we said, "that comparisons are odious. She was talking about Mrs. Mortar, a neighbor mother, who was always comparing her son Johnny Mortar to our temperamental brother. But we can see how what she said might have something to do with the sea."

The memory of Johnny Mortar and his mother, Midge Mortar, had come to mind very suddenly, and we remembered the smell of their dachshund on rainy days when Mrs. Mortar would persuade us to come over for cookies and then tie us to a chair and tickle us.

"Is remembering at all like fishing," we asked, leading up to something.

"I'll let you compare them for yourself," the mate said.

Already this is endless.

> beauty floating beauty floating
> the surface of the sea is roaring

We enjoyed the marine activity immensely. We discovered that remembering is not like fishing, any more than forgetting is like fucking. And Mama was right that comparisons put someone at a disadvantage, and this someone could very well be someone's temperamental brother. Our conversation, overlapping the things at sea and the movement of things within, amused the mate. He laughed, and asked us to cook some rice and spice it with pickles, declaring that we were certainly nobody's brother.

"That's a sexist request," we said.

This provoked a big amorous response.

>     thousands of smudges
>     not all from memory—
>     what else occurs in a flash

Things on deck were busy, the fishing boat was bouncing, the fish
were coming in, and the mate was suddenly blushing. "I apologize,"
he said. "Really."

We softened.

>     ice
>     winter
>     ice
>     or
>     not
>
>     smudged
>     city ice
>
>     the wall falls and floods

the tongue

on

the roof

is gritty

and jelly


a steaming wall among feet


just under

the cheek

a hand

pelts

rains

parts


within broken synonyms


I

me

you

they

us

and

she

he

Those were some of the smudges organized on the smudged surfaces, folded inside some memories, which were in turn entwined in comforting habits of organization while wars met on each side of their beginnings and endings.

And people follow wars—certain people, titillated by the almost medically sanctified certainly medically ritualized televised preparations.

      sacrifice

      paradise

      scrape the pudding

      liberalize

      make the gutting

      more and moralize

      ape the studding

      appetize

      infantilize

A general was on television. He touched a pointer to a map. "This is a member nation," he said in a low emotional voice.

The contrast between violence and the tranquility of the photo was almost religious.

We vomited.

We were excused.

We left Rocky Welf in a rented two-door car.

> a clue is only a buttonhole
> the button in turn is cajoled
> o man(sic)kind, get wide

A red tulip the size of a dinner plate with a scent is for sale. We pull up to the nursery in our rented car.

"We haven't received our bulbs yet, but I know nothing of the tulip you speak of," says the gardener.

There is something peculiar about the nursery. It seems unremittingly sexual. We conclude we have never seen a flower until this moment. It is as if each plant opens and closes for us. Why did they have a life of their own before? Then the speckled perky plants hugging the ground appear to be backing away from us. To them we are a sexual monster spilling our eyes onto their tiny throats.

Some flowers bow their heads in longing. We are referring particularly to a modest star-like gladiola, a single flower bent at the tip of an emerald stem. Clearly it silently hungers to brush its face against our open hands.

> it longs
> to handle
> our commands
> with soft ears
> dancing around
> sword spinning fins

This great pleasure in power pollinates our face until it seems as large as a dinner plate. We cup our blooming nose, smack our over-hydrated lips, pinch our mud-leached eyes. Our legs are twining passion vines. Their whirligig blossoms sip our stemmy juices and quietly pilot themselves into cup and saucer emptiness. A monstrous swamp gut power pours out of us. With our entrails inside out and outside in and in and in, we wonder how in Ovid's name we got here.

the plate

the lips

the tulips

and a kiss

were meant

for undermining

the duplicitous

state

"We got here through the rear," we say laughingly to the inquiring rose who then remarks, disdainfully, that she keeps as far away from swamps as possible, and since she can't move herself, perhaps we could remove ourself to the lily pond where she is sure the dragonflies are dying to meet us.

"Yes, fine, we're on our way," we say, "but can you just tell us one thing, do any of the dragonflies go by either the name of Donald Duck or Schwarzkopf?"[2]

Her leaves pale to a vomity green. Rust inches its way up the tips. Her head drops over and the petals fall instantly. Yet, even

---

2    General H. Norman Schwarzkopf (meaning 'black head' in German) was the leader of the American forces during "Desert Storm," the massive assault on Iraq following Iraq's invasion of Kuwait in 1989.

without her persona, her thorns glisten and raise the hackles of the surrounding foliage.

> yes, they are shouting
> penstemon
> of the bearded tongue
> as if this were the key
> to Schwarzkopf

Aching with knowledge, like dirt farmers on dark ground, we know that plucking is never final. We are in a transitional zone here, unpossessed and unpossessing.

There are certain places—inhabited sites, populated locations—that can be mobilized, transported in lives, and re-established—Italy to Little Italy, Russia to Little Russia—but empty places remain where they are. Wyoming, for example, can't be moved. And it's a place where it's hard to garden.

But we arouse flowers.

"What you pluck here is bound to disappear," as they say on the occasional morbid billboard that has not been destroyed by the ecological knight known as the Green Fox. His motto, rumored but nowhere inscribed, was "Set Undeclared Precedents." We could see this would lead to cycles.

We know cycles. We also know ripples and topples. Each in its place, we say.

We have romantic and real desires. These are logical eroticisms.

We can merge more than we already have.

> a saturating thought
> of shadows

We like to have sex outdoors in the sun where the sun can see into our pants. We pull ourself a little open. This feels a little daring, a little unabashed, a little fertile, and it's all of these. The sunlight begins to focus on us, the colors swirl and converge, the heat on us increases, even burns slightly between our legs, as the sun looks in.

## FORAY

Let's imagine that desire invites perceptions, mediating the interplay of sensation with knowledge. And let's imagine a distant barking mobilizing a dog. It was on its way to the next world or a feast, was it not? The acrid smell of a wet dog can be reassuring and it can complicate things. Will it be welcome when it gets there?

No, the dog was not going to a feast. It was in its own world. And it is necessary to speak of ferns as well. Myriad ants crawl through the fern

## ARRAY

Too often curtailed! Too often abandoned! Too often speechless! Why measure desire? But have we now even approached it or seen it or known it?

This is the reason to measure desire even without realistic implements: to safeguard its prevalence.

Our task is paradoxical and ornamentally sexual. On the one hand, there is no measuring implement: neither a tadpole, nor world whose denizens tickle our ankles. We enter one place without having to leave everything behind us.

No, thanks to desires and perceptions we get to be in multiple worlds. But we like the idea of there being things left behind and things in our way. And yes, all the courses for the feast are on the table at once. There are puddings and pomegranate salad, roasted halibut, sugar cookies, hydrangea blossoms *en croute*, and the wobbling flames of four dozen candles. A saffron chicken and deviled eggs with capers. Ramekins with red and ochre sauces.

The boyfriend of the pudding chef collects photographs with themes.

Remember how excited he was when he discovered the abandoned albums beside the dumpster on Tenth Street? In them were photographs of bill-

a flagpole, nor a ruler; although, the tadpole is an image of impregnation, a flagpole something to sit on top of, victoriously and even salaciously, and a ruler always good for a swat. On the other hand, even the mention of desire causes desire to commence measuring itself and its implements of measurement are as various as the imagination.

But be careful: some of the usages of measure are more elegant than others. Those that start out with a series of discrete and formal gestures are sometimes those that provide the context for the greatest improvised abandon. A word carefully placed can erect a nipple. How high?

We are greasing our palms with palm grease before we count our lovers, those who grease our recollections.

boards, windmills, and bridges, the same images printed on the name cards at the feast. These are conversation pieces, clearly useful when strangers from long distances mingle.

A guest from Bridgeton asks about someone with mismatched boots. "That's the botanist we wish you to get to know," says the host. "How kind, how generous and thoughtful. I've been looking for an expert," replies the guest.

Ferns grow under the table, pricking our ankles with their delicate spikes. A brook flows through them, spreading wider and wider. Tadpoles sport in its eddies. The moon makes her appearance, and frogs sing lines from the poet Lucha Corpi:

Vivo con el estomago aqui
y el corazon al otro lado del rio

Rooms fill up with each other. The eucalyptus, the must, the piss, the sweet grass, and pastiche of the rooms fill the recollections as we grease our palms to count our lovers. Let us not, however, deceive anyone into thinking that counting lovers is a measure of desire. Measuring desire is never a quantifying of lovers, although sometimes we imagine them all in the same room together as a substitute for a furnace in winter.

Desire measures itself in the distance, between itself and its object, which advances and is always advancing within time. All the way through all the climaxes it continues its strategies, even when curtailed, abandoned, and without words.

But what of regret, that form of hindsight which is an erotic

*(I live with my stomach here*
*and my heart on the other side of the river)*

Speaking of experts, she knows a lot. Yes, yes. The poet figures the words, has had her day in court, has made offerings to the public, and all the way round—even behind the scenes—is someone to look up to, is she not?

But how does the frog know her song? It's one of the mysteries, isn't it? The nervous sounds of amphibians resemble a vale of words we attempt to interpret, find reason in, but do we really understand the message?

Does one really want the answer? Perhaps not, because the answer is close to no. What is the difference between a frog's song and a poem? Or us and amphibians?

punishment, an exacerbator, the one that makes us plot? We enjoy the sweet bitterness of drama— come to me my darling in a bath of furs—as long as it doesn't stay too close to our passage from here to there.

Missed occasions, shortened visits, interruptions—. These indicate a geography of emotions that can get on our nerves when we encounter too many of them. You know that abridged wandering of the dead soul when it loses track of time? It haunts us a little in a grove of bay trees, where we encounter its remorseful scent. Ferns cluster below in a tumultuous ravine. Beyond several sets of switchbacks and stairs is a view of a town we feel we know too well. It is not yet time to return to the proper world. We sit on a

It's no sin to live with divided desires. We can couple body and soul, and a loquacious forest with a postal annex. We can couple almost any one thing with another.

Is that what Lucha Corpi is performing in these lines? Listen, the stomach is here: one becomes fond of its sounds. Empty, full, empty, full, empty, full.

Words, choking off the access to water. It's melancholy I know, but as I speak this I can see the poet's lips parting. She swallows back some tears, and the lips close. The stomach growls. Hunger is in two places at once.

In "This Lime Tree Bower My Prison," Coleridge, immobilized by an injured ankle, takes in his imagination a walk he had been eagerly anticipating to a river with others. Here am I, he says, tree stump peering hopefully at an empty corral.

Beyond there, rewarded, we straddled a rental pony and relentlessly rode uphill against a flow of pedestrians lugging shopping bags. A woman in high-heeled straw shoes pulled a banana from a satchel. While reading a text message, a little girl lapped at a pineapple cone. Our pinto rental pony tossed its mane, zigzagging through the barreling crowd. We slowed in front of a man who was reaching into the back pocket of his jeans. Without warning, he lurched toward us and jabbed a notebook at the head of the pinto pony.

A feather from a floppy yellow hat fell between its pages. It spoke of our copulating with Great Danes. A policeman whistled. While taking saddened by his singularity. Then the scene changes.

Ought we then to leave the concerns of the stomach behind? This is one of those questions that can be best answered by considering the particulars of the situation.

Two crows are mobilized and swoop into the air. Healthy as pigs and fat as bananas they fly toward a pine tree, landing on adjacent branches.

All of this love talk with experts is a risky thing.

But we might have remained silent, lolling alone as if we were pencils recording the tales of a lovelorn anthropologist.

A sincere smile is covered by a hand holding a match. A sincere smile is

possession of the book, we acknowledged him with a shrug, waggled our fingertips, but didn't stop.

The pony seemed tireless, but when we turned abruptly into Furrow Street, the pinto bucked. We fell like almonds tumbling from a counter, landing in a fallow field. It might have been intended for onions. Or for artichokes, we couldn't know.

Such things are a nuisance but there's nothing here to regret. True or false are only applicable to what's knowable, and knowledge is only applicable to what's happened.

Yesterday a man ran his fingers through our hair, but his train arrived. He could have taken a later train, but we failed to tell him so. We regret this, but only incrementally, through stages of initiation, measured covered by match light and emissions from a fluorescent tube. The screen heats up, emits the blues. This is a harsh depiction missing certain details. Glasses left on a shelf. Eyes erring in the view of someone. It's not who was expected after all. Adjust the lens. It's only a click of a shutter, an instruction to look again.

No clock time, no furnishings. The flash of an idea, the surprise of its dissolve, the tree in the window, the profile slips. Is it that we are *in* or *at* the film? It feels like one but in fact it's neither. Here's the camera silently recording a dove with the crunch of spilled cereal underfoot in the empty room.

Destination: as advertised.

The photograph of a bridge spanning a wide river gathers illimitable silence on a surface of light. Grasses according to the time it takes to wish for something and then to act on it.

And what of loneliness born of regret? We are an unusual creature, since we are set apart from loneliness compositionally, even though we, like others, suffer unexpected losses and our own inexact finitude.

A doorway was half made. Did it protect an interior space or define an enclosed space? Our protagonist, who stepped through the half-finished doorway, bumped right into a man with whom she fell unmistakably and irrevocably in love.

He was not particularly great to look at but rather a hodgepodge of many others whom she had admired in the past, with his short greying hair, a gawkingly awkward height, and an uninspired mustache. When he spoke, she was certain he was a bending and rebounding, bending and rebounding.

An angular barge passing under a concrete rail-and-slab bridge over gray churning water. A scrolling of sporadic silence and light.

In the flickering projection a lighthouse appears, its beam scans and finds something too far off for us, sprawling low in our seat, to discern. The beam passes over the racing cyclists now crossing the bridge.

A bridge, flick, a span.

A span, flick: a mast. Water. Fish in murky light. A woman. We see her mouth open and foresee her shout in the silence: "I want something. I want it now. I want it from *you!*"

We watch her lips in search of the name of the desirable object. Unlike

mathematician and when she touched his hand she experienced a universe being sucked into her body, bouncing and mingling in her sex with limitless teasing, tickles, and ostentatious pressures. Now, with every increment of motion within, her desire to expel the inhaled universe into an explosion of song sliding down the strings of a viola through the coal-ridden creases of earth rocketing back out in flame and river-lashing liquid became exaggerated. He was as surprised as she by this. There seemed to be nothing to say, but he did want to know when he could see her next. She tried to remember what had been going on the minute before she'd met this man.

A boulder crashed down the side of the eastern hills behind them. As the eastern hills gave way to a force or weakness no one had anticipated, the man, the woman, and others a photograph, a film can't serve as a memento.

It could if it were short enough. And if it didn't take so much equipment to make it perceptible.

But a film buff can show herself a film from her personal DVD collection at will.

And it is with willfulness that the woman in the film is shouting out her demand for the desirable object whose name we can't ascertain. It looks like "lamb field" or "lady fern."

She is mouthing something with intent. We are watching with more than anthropological interest. The figure of the woman merges with that of a carved wood fetish adorned with eucalyptus leaves, a single horse's tooth, and scraps of robin breast.

ran for their lives, climbing to the high ground of the northern mesas. Although the woman could see the avalanche, she could no longer discern the details. Like a detached observer in a dream, she wondered if there'd been injury to people and their houses.

The man led her to a building. They climbed some stairs and entered a room of beds, full of sleeping children covered in orange, red, and brown comforters. They were a snorting, noisy group of sleepers.

The man, perhaps out of embarrassment, said nothing, but there was nothing that could restrain her from unbuttoning his blouse.

The man was like Rousseau in that he measured his inspiration according to the scales of nature and exposed

The terraced theater with its slanted floor is an oneiric enclosure. It's a pen at the top of a staircase. The teacher is at her desk; the students are in bed in pajamas. We are surveying the back of a pickup truck, we gaze at a rosy glass desk, a mechanical tickling toy, a clothesline on which corsets and panties are hanging to dry in the radiant silver sunlight.

We are being subjected to an experiment in changing emotional states. But it's our own experiment, isn't it? We dreamed it up. And we remembered something.

"When a man's glance is following certain household preparations, especially those for a meal, there is apt to be a look on his face that combines religious attention, boredom, and fear." That's Colette.

himself to nature's danger, but he was unlike Rousseau in that he had children about, whereas Rousseau had deposited each of his children at infancy in an orphanage.

The man was like Sade in that the grunting functioning polymorphic sleeping scene exacted from him not discretion but abandon—a wild and extreme acquiescence—so that he, a voracious naturalist, might slide into nothingness.

The man was like Madame de Sévigné in that he was an empirical observer who adored to relate the details around him in handwritten letters to cousins abroad and to neighbors.

Regret, a sensuous deferral of communication, precedes letters.

Let's remember the place in the woods where we stopped to compare a shrubby ravine extending uphill under leaning tree trunks with certain landscape paintings by Cézanne in which the background steps out from behind the trees. In the ravine there were gaudy berries. Carefully we parted the brambles to pick them.

Desirous observation flows through our memory with irrational devotion. Desirous observation flows by as we remember the prick of the brambles growing in the gently eroded ravine framed by the diagonal trunks of tall dry pines. The silence, afloat here in the light of retrospect, folds around the languorous buzzing of a fly somewhere among the berries.

Let's replace the berries with dimpled rubber objects.

Loneliness is nothing, encompassing abandon.

In loneliness the past seems vast.

As a wife has said, it often seems that the husband is lost in the grass.

Something, meanwhile, is keeping us from speaking to a phantom. Did we think that things stand still?

If we don't watch the sun move, nothing happens—nothing repeats—nothing persists.

The lonely woman of our profession has written her way into a romance, and she floats away in a wisp of thought leaving us holding our hands on the wide road.

A feather pokes at our neck, reminding us that we've not yet read

It feels like memory, a language of you-me, girls holding hands quiet as fish in the noisy brook. We were the Romantics, we liked the Romantics. Coleridge was a monster. Add the still of his hand and the other of his handwriting. These resemble fissures in a dramatic landscape.

And now the camera moves to the water, tilts down and fuses the shadows of the two girls. They are charming, monstrous, buried between mossy rocks, looking in. Sticks passing over the warp of outfits floating up. Their bodies are waving hands, all wave and floating dummies. Smiles wiped away by the ripples birds induce diving at bugs flying upstream just above the surface of shooting light.

How did the protagonist get there? There's no telling. The film screen goes black. Are we looking or the book we appropriated on the pony ride.

It appears to be a diary. The air is warm, eddies of humidity are stirred by bees.

10/6 Tolerable heat. But heat nonetheless. Rejected Tim in an irrigation ditch. Now I am climbing the walls of my inner strength.

10/8 Saw Philip from a distance. I am on top of the wall. Waiting for the fall.

10/9 Fell.

10/11 The sun at its peak competes with his comforting moans.

11/6 Philip is gone, sick of competing with the universe for my affections.

11/7 The universe is intolerant of my needs. Menstrual bleeding shooting? In the black a dump truck noise, benign urban rumbles. A story of survival enters with tears and a lot of talk, barking, chatter. The lens opens on burning sun. It appears to burn its way through the surface of the screen of the eye. It's a trick of military genius learned on a desert set. A piece of paper crumbles, smoking as an illustration of what is always happening. Silence is everywhere, because the sound has been left out. Each soldier wants respect and to be left to do a job properly. This is a serious scene and we don't figure in it.

It's like a little sentence in human history found in Coleridge's handwriting. Thus the reflection in the mirror that comes next. Two women opening their mouths, possibly sharing makeup. Someone, something, coming up on them from

reminds me that I may not care about any of this tomorrow. But I never can believe it.

11/8 More symptomatics and I will forget everything. I still prefer the universe to Philip, even though my cavities are filled with extra holes.

11/9 Philip says he is willing to play second fiddle.

11/10 I tell him he has to play third: to the universe and then to my theoretical writings. He says I am only saying this to humble him.

12/4 These entries seem to be getting closer together. When I wrote that last one, I must have been secretly arguing with him. Now I ask myself this question, do I want to humiliate him?

behind. You can see the shadow in the mirror, the women pause, close and open the eyes.

Cut to an empty room and sound on. Uninterpretable, diffuse shuffling. An exit and a pan. We see the room is a mock-up on a little table in what appears to be a quite ordinary backyard. Two girls enter from nowhere talking up a storm. When they arrive at the table one of them picks up the little mock-up and places it in the hand of the other child. The other child blows on it as if it were a dandelion and the walls fly open. On the hand of one child rests a little piece of cardboard sprinkled with a few flecks of cereal. The children share the grain.

Two women enter again from somewhere unstated, as if they have no place of origin. They investigate the table. Something is missing. It

12/5 I want to reorchestrate 'the social fabric' by forcing him to recognize my priorities. I want to know what it feels like to succeed symbolically, although I fear nagging emptiness.

It's in the very nature of a journal of separated and abandoned moments to let us forget them and then to represent them back to us.

We desire abandon, of course, because desiring it serves as a prelude to desiring the critical reunion of detail. We love detail because we wish to suspend the universal.

Fact:

> Under unusually copious spring rain, the hillsides and city lots are deep in grass.

Logic:

> The more the grass grows, the more the rain falls.

doesn't seem to be the girls but it's possibly the little mock-up of the room. They look under the table and on the ground, finally becoming self-conscious. Is it because they are aware of being watched or does the activity somehow seem unflattering or guilty? They are each now standing at either end of the table looking at one another laughing. "We're always doing the same thing." And the other says, "That's what *you* think." And they burst out in laughter again, doubled over.

"I can hardly remember why we were looking."

"Were we looking for something?"

They laugh more and more. One of them sits on the ground holding her stomach. The other takes off her sandal, gesturing as if she's about

Fact:

Tim is a cardiologist.

Logic:

Since every heart is surrounded by something animal, Tim may be a moose.

Fact:

A man in a russet canoe drifts toward us; his skin is dark, his eyes are dark, he is reading a dark book; it is Philip.

Logic:

Men seem to stare at women but they don't learn much.

Fact:

In response to Philip's disgruntlement, we will undertake a formidable task.

to throw it. A piece of cardboard slips off the sandal onto the table as she lets go of the sandal which flies past the head of the laughing seated woman. They both dive for the sandal like little children at play, struggling over a toy gun.

When sensation is aroused creatures forage.

Our monstrous nature puts ourself in a position to remain open to refusal. We keep a few secrets in our bag. The midwife pulls something out in a story that has to be written. But who would be willing to write it?

This would possibly be something monstrous.

This is the monstrous baby.

Logic:

Full of the refreshing joy of liberation, travel permits one to taste with one's whole being.

Subsidiary logic:

Nighttime though it is
The performers, scopic—
Is the river visible today?

Logical terms:

*Absence*

*And*

*Beauty*

*Camera*

*Copula*

(see *And*; see *Copulation*)

*Copulation*

(see *Camera*)

*Desire*

*Experience*

*Form*

(*see Beauty*)

*Measure*

The story? Whose future we become? As Zora Neale Hurston writes, "We have memories within that come out of the material that goes to make us." The result is commitment, not fulfillment.

But first, there's a back-story full of dirty knowledge. Sensations, circulated in broadsides.

Look, the baby is having a great time, quite fulfilled actually, isn't that so?

Well, that depends on warring interests and property laws. Where are these things going to fit?

There is no fitting room.

That's not what I mean.

Were you referring to corporate interests? Or…

*Vice*

*We*

*Zoology*

   (see *Beauty*, *Form*,

   and *Measure*)

Emotional terms:

   nighttime.time.subordination. allegory. descent. journey.

Logic:

   When one starts out on a journey, one is scripted by an idea, therefore becoming subordinate to the idea. The subordinate creature offers her body as both domicile and vehicle for the fulfillment of the idea, which requires another party, Action. Action and Idea are as contiguous as the trajectory of partners executing a business plan. If Idea bosses Action around

No, just warring ones.

Pedestrians arrive at the aberrant hybridity and part to avoid it. That makes for a lot more action.

You're referring to the lines on the hand the palmist studies. She can't see the past because our hand doesn't give her the right information. The lines of the past are effaced.

There's something manifest that can't be read. Not even by the clairvoyant Florinda Gable, whom we met on the bus in Saint Louis.

The pedestrians, in parting and creating all that activity, replicate the thing they fear in a different form. In the annals of monstrosity we find an aberrant cockatoo, an empowered potato. They become human and scatter.

now, she will receive an earful of narrative later upon Action's return from the field. It is then Idea's turn to condense the narrative into a strategy to further fulfillment of the plan. (A suited man with gray beard and steaming coffee is staring at us in the café as we endeavor to compose an allegory in the image of our retinue).

Emotion:

She is inscribed in a language that incites sexual violence. (Idea and Action invade the body of an unsuspecting host.)

An erotic quest can manufacture nightmares as well as nightlife or the sun rising perennially in dishabille. What it must not do is betray the pleasure of address. (Dear Para Nelly Days Abby). Or

Let's volunteer for duty in the part of a story about just getting by. Unobtrusively. A costume, adapting to current trends.

What no one will know as we wheel our cart courteously through the aisles of the supermarket is that we will dine on potatoes grown in paradise covered with butter given us by a youth responding to our pen scratching on the skin of a mango into whose flesh we have pressed our clitoris.

The story has accomplished what it set out to do, trampling something vulnerable underfoot, yet the monster is still here, foraging.

We could frighten the boys with such knowledge, but for now let's save it in our bag, along with the pointed dibble. We can put pressure on pleasure again later.

the incongruous. Let us consider the adventure of the necrophiliac and the chaste kissy doll: we offer each of them nectar, to test the properties of the drink. If it bestows immortality on each of them, they will survive our story. Death, sex, narration, and chastity will be inextricably linked. One hundred years hence, the reader of this book will envision the kissy doll recoiling in horror at the necrophiliac's rejection of her. The necrophiliac will wade through her prayers each night, waiting for the kissy doll to die. This will go on eternally, and will always be a stopping point on the wide road; however, if the nectar does not bestow immortality on the kissy doll and the necrophiliac, we will buy plots for them in a local necropolis and leave a space for some other story to replace them. In the meantime, the underground brook has jettisoned

Measured though the world is not, the distance has moved very close. Each grass blade is a monument to structure. And with this in mind we arrive at Sunday, a breakfast on the lawn, a perspective, a pronouncement, and a promenade of slurps. An investigation of leisure is underway, which, when pressed into small increments, is also pressed into the esoteric zones between fingers, toes, lips, blades, and lines of verse.

Dear Reader, if you've had too much languor, or language, if it bores you now, skip over this part or take a break. Have you seen *Transformers: Revenge of the Fallen*? Interject its clamor into this extension of our desire to waste time.

Our foray continues with the dream of the most voluptuous bodies in baroque scenes, but now in present our image of ourself, which lies damp and torpid on the bank of a tossed off business arrangement.

No emotion is the last one. Writing the sentence at the suggestion of our story—at night but without night panic (that form of mirthless sanity which requires an explanation for everything)—we *feel* that we cannot divide past emotions from future emotions and we *feel* the spread of the present as we move right foot to right and left foot to left in the spread of the bed.

Night time, time, subordination, allegory, descent, and journey. Night time inspires subjectivity; time sets the stage for revolution; subordination knocks logic, that lonely domino, on its back so that love, enamored of its dots, may rub them one by one; allegory protime, lounging nude on a suburban lawn. When we arrive dressed in untidy curls, the hosts take us to the backyard and introduce us to their entrepreneurial family, famous for their advertisements of blue condoms that come in many hues and have names like Sacred C, Deep Blue Sea, Cerulean Pane, Sky Way, Faint, Cobalt Finish, Navy Harp, Sapphire Cream, Azure Me, Filthy Clean.

A sea of tangled, floating, lounging bodies extends across the acreage on a canopy of faded blankets. We enjoy the edge of a blanket we have been offered to sit on.

The thought of curls reminds us not to forget hard bodies. While twirling our finger through a lock of hair, we are distracted by a ladybug perched on our navel. Dislodging the bug on a finger, we lift it and it flies into a cluster of strewn acorns in the longs logic's nocturnal descent into the bed of subjectivity; descent is synonymous with interiorization but the place where it arrives is somewhere else, somewhere out there where we, on waking, find ourself on foot and underway, making progress; and journey. Action takes will, will takes imagination, imagination takes doubt, doubt takes action.

The domino effect that we are experiencing in our logic means that we haven't been able to hurry our journey. Like Stoics we have separated cause from effect.

And so we carry out our confatalia, whose history is one of exposed conjugation. Our body is a fantasy of a baffling meeting in a meadow, a stanza occasioning a violent though tender shudder, a wreath of perspiration under a hat.

grass just beyond our extended feet. Now on hands and knees we approach the tiny creature.

Minutiae are voracious and broody, we've been told. With our ass in the air, we peer closer. A blade of grass tickles our cheek. A breath of unexpectedly warm air wafts across our forehead. We find ourself eye to eye with a blurry face looming before us.

Don't move, it says. To reproduce one's kind in the undergrowth of intimate relations requires long-term, small-scale scurrying followed by longish passages of time. Each seedpod is a monument to formal reorganization.

The hum of his voice catches us up in the microscopic world of which he seems to be an expert. How do you know all this? we whisper. His tongue slides over his lower lip, which is

In the morning, a morning man is there. He's as real as a lip and we write in our notebook:

corner paper wits near nervy glands
satellite rice-paddy step next
on a rock
out on fit little stage
form-resonance of poetry's lips

twist our legs, inside and around
paddy step
filthy pants pocket down
goes on fit pale peninsula
stains, ghostly pause on foreground

moon-viewing
paddy fingers sun float
to the very end of dusty earth ease
eight syllables derive goose grass
as they say

enlarged by a small magnifying glass he is holding in front of his face. He rotates the glass and holds it over the ladybug. All around it are ants scuttling between sheaves of grass and over the acorns.

The structure of intimate relations in the undergrowth is a slow predacious flow.

Sounds like the marriage form of sexual culture, we whisper.

Perhaps, he says. Some insects insert their eggs into the bodies of the larvae of another insect. When the eggs hatch they eat the larvae up. And look at the oaks, he says rising. Into the canker goes a blue butterfly pupa, out comes a fledged red wasp.

A vague, lascivious sensation of egginess and insertion, minute insinuations, some slapping and plunging

where the legs light over
sun as another sound we summer
arguing a thousand summons
to derive
without wild composing

this stretch of chance off the road aways
another sun of different nights
to take in
or derive or fasten
we jotted down these conversations

scribbling     on     our     hat     sideways
        through a field
as  other  pleasure  signs  travel  the
        same way

There's no escape from our response—that's for sure. Just now, we desire an innocence associated with garden beds and are finding it between our knees. Or, we will have it in the moment, with the morning man running the bird feather over our lips.

comes over the party. Things are heating up. We too rub the sun between our legs. It comes with some dirt and scratchy edges of fallen oak leaves.

We sprawl across the landscape fantasy of sexuality comprised of sucks, nuts, pheromone-demented ants, spider legs running between breasts. Can we call this natural?

Not if we change spider legs to spider fingers. And not if those elements we've drawn into the fantasy are derived from a beautifully photographed documentary whose corpulent narrator frequently sticks his forefinger into holes in the ground, probing for life forms to observe. He could not disguise his religious enthusiasm, which for a little while we had ardently shared.

But now, have we not each done enough basic service? And Sunday soon comes to an end.

Migrating sensations recall to mind that two sides of a river never overlap. Yet bubbles follow brain paths. Our memories of undulating water exist even as our feet find the solid ground that's there, regardless of our disposition. But somehow our feet seem to be getting larger and larger, our legs too. And the lines of a hand have become tropical ravines. Several other hands are blooming with gorges and canyons. Our fingers sprout cineplexes and hospitals: one with a bamboo motif shelters veterans. And here our navel adorns Plato's cave with a neo-classical casing, while our vagina accommodates the proverbial railway station it has sometimes been compared to. To be enormous is a wish that comes over us in our hot desperation. Then, miraculously, everything on earth swells to our proportions.

*The Wide Road* was collaboratively composed by Carla Harryman and Lyn Hejinian between 1991 and 2010. The cover art was drawn for this manuscript by the artist Nancy Blum in the summer of 2010. The first edition is printed in a run of 1000 with two cover designs by HR Hegnauer. The type is set in Perpetua and Gill Sans.

A webpage of critical conversation and story about this book can be found at: www.belladonnaseries.org/thewideroad.html

Belladonna Books is a publication project of the Belladonna* Collaborative, a multi-dimensional mobilization of feminist avant-garde writing.

www.belladonnaseries.org

# green
# press
INITIATIVE

Belladonna Books is committed to preserving ancient forests and natural resources. We elected to print this title on 30% postconsumer recycled paper, processed chlorine-free. As a result, we have saved:

3 Trees (40' tall and 6-8" diameter)
1 Million BTUs of Total Energy
300 Pounds of Greenhouse Gases
1,447 Gallons of Wastewater
88 Pounds of Solid Waste

Belladonna Books made this paper choice because our printer, Thomson-Shore, Inc., is a member of Green Press Initiative, a nonprofit program dedicated to supporting authors, publishers, and suppliers in their efforts to reduce their use of fiber obtained from endangered forests.

For more information, visit www.greenpressinitiative.org

Environmental impact estimates were made using the Environmental Defense Paper Calculator. For more information visit: www.edf.org/papercalculator